HEATHROW AIRPORT

HEATHROW AIRPORT

AN ILLUSTRATED HISTORY

KEVAN JAMES

FONTHILL

Fonthill Media Language Policy

Fonthill Media publishes in the international English language market. One language edition is published worldwide. As there are minor differences in spelling and presentation, especially with regard to American English and British English, a policy is necessary to define which form of English to use. The Fonthill Policy is to use the form of English native to the author. Kevan James was born and educated in Cyprus and now lives in Kent; British English has therefore been adopted in this publication.

Fonthill Media Limited
Fonthill Media LLC
www.fonthillmedia.com
office@fonthillmedia.com

First published in the United Kingdom and the United States of America 2016

British Library Cataloguing in Publication Data:
A catalogue record for this book is available from the British Library

Copyright © Kevan James 2016

ISBN 978-1-78155-511-8

Typeset in 10pt on 13pt Sabon
Printed and bound in England

Foreword

I was not born for one corner—the whole world is my native land.

Seneca

Legend has it that Dick Turpin used to linger around these parts, waiting for a horse-drawn coach to trundle by on its way from London to Staines and the south west, at which point he would block the road, stop the coach and—politely or otherwise— remove money and valuables from the unfortunate traveller.

It may be that the legend is a product of the fertile imagination of the story-teller and movie-maker, as there is no real evidence to suggest Turpin did actually ply his illicit trade here (although others of similar tendencies may well have done). The bleak emptiness of Hounslow Heath certainly gave ample opportunity to commit highway robbery for those of a mind to do so.

Well before this time, much of the forest on either side of the road had been cleared— first by the Romans, who built a characteristically straight road from London to Staines, and then, in the thirteenth century, by King Henry III. The king created a heath—a flat stretch of open land—running from Staines to Brentford. It was an impressive undertaking, and one that would prove to be of great benefit to the king's descendants.

Slightly further north, the Bath Road was the route of the ancient Great West Road. Another king, George III, along with dignitaries of the time, travelled between London and Windsor Castle using the road. During the summer of 1784, the road to Bath would probably have been used by Major-General William Roy FRS RE as, just south of it, he measured a survey baseline across Hounslow Heath; the purpose was to determine the relative positions of the Greenwich Observatory and *L'Observatoire de Paris*, measuring the distance between them. The two ends of this baseline were marked by contemporary military cannon set in the ground, with their muzzles facing upward. Roy's advocacy and leadership led to the creation of the Ordnance Survey in 1971, the year after his death. Roy would more likely have used Cain's Lane, which stretched south from the Great West road across the heath until it met the Great Southwest Road, where Dick Turpin is alleged to have committed his crimes.

One of the earliest settlements in the area was marked on Roy's maps as 'Caesar's Camp', although there is nothing concrete to suggest that either Caesar himself or any other Roman built anything permanent here. In 1906, the site was levelled and ploughed over as agriculture became the main reason for people to live here. The plough took its toll on much of the heath, with only a few acres south of the Roman Road still remaining as open land.

Today the area is unrecognizable from its early days. Instead of the vast expanse of heath and trees and the occasional hamlet around its edges, it is now the site of one of the world's busiest airports—Heathrow. It is the United Kingdom's primary hub of international air travel. Only six airports in the world have direct, non-stop, long-haul flights to more than fifty destinations, and Heathrow is one of them.

Since 1 January 1946, when the first departure to South America took off, Heathrow has welcomed the world to London and to Great Britain. The pace of its growth over its seven decades has been such that there has never been a time that some kind of building work has not been going on somewhere within the airport's boundaries—work needed to improve, develop, and redevelop and enlarge the facilities for the constantly growing number of passengers and the airlines that carry them.

Nevertheless, Heathrow has aroused passionate debate almost since the day it opened. During the years immediately prior the airport's seventieth birthday in 2016, arguments raged against expanding it by adding a third runway; the airport originally had six. To build Terminal 5 took years of public planning inquiries in the face of objections from those who stood against the airport. The process became the longest in UK history, but the terminal was built. Even before the first layout designs had been drawn, the creation of Heathrow took some subterfuge and sleight of hand—but it was built.

Despite the arguments for and against Heathrow, the now physically cramped airport site, and the never-ending building and improvement cycle, the airport functions, and it has seen many great and historic events. Heathrow has been the point of departure and arrival for millions of people, and its impact cannot be understated.

Events such as Heathrow's seventieth anniversary do not happen that frequently, and even though my own seven-decade milestone is still some distance away, I can say that I have grown up with Heathrow—at least in the modern era.

This book includes a chronicle of Heathrow's seventy years and is a personal portrayal of the airport throughout a big part of my life, alongside a more intimate view through the eyes of just a very few of the thousands (perhaps, after all these years, the hundreds of thousands) of people whose working lives revolved around it, and those who have been, and still are, enthusiastic about it.

Kevan James

Rochester, England
2016

Acknowledgements

There are several people who helped me enormously when I was writing *Heathrow: An Illustrated History*. Without them, the book would not be complete.

In no particular order, I would like to thank Colin Dobbs, David Winyard, Fay Jordan, Leo Martin, Micky, Clive, and Neil Martin, Keith Gilchrist, Richard Briggs, Simon Boddy, Steve Hopwood, Tony Horton, Tyler McDowell, and Stephan Parfitt. I would especially like to thank the Fonthill team for having faith and putting up with me, and Mark Nicholls, Craig West, and Andy Martin for giving me a break.

Contents

Glossary

Wherever I go, I'm watching ... when I'm in an airport ... I look around, snap pictures, and find out how people do things.

Richard Scarry

Aviation is full of technical terms that can confuse not only the uninitiated but sometimes even those who work in the industry. This book contains a few, so I've listed and defined some of them here. Hopefully, this will leave those not *au-fait* with the terminology less likely to indulge in mystified head-scratching.

Ailerons, Flaps and Slats

Aircraft wings are really rather complex constructions. The wings keep the aircraft in the air and contain a terrifyingly large amount of jet fuel, and hanging off them, on most modern airliners, are the engines. Either side of the engines are the parts that extend for take-off and landing, which are almost as long as the wings themselves. The slats are the long, thin bits that extend from the front (or 'leading edge') of the wing, and the flaps extend from the back (or 'trailing edge'). Both provide additional lift, thus keeping the aircraft flying even at slow speeds. Aircraft can take off and land without the slats and flaps out, but it's not recommended and there are various settings. It can be fatal to take off with the slats and flaps extended but not correctly set.

Airbridge

Also known as 'Jetways' in the USA, these are the long, telescoping, enclosed walkways used to board aircraft and disembark from them to get to terminal gates. They are handy when it's raining.

Airport Three-letter Designators

All airports have a three-letter code that identifies them in aviation-speak (there is also a four-letter code, but we needn't worry about them since only the three-letter codes are used in this book). Before Gatwick became London's second airport, the UK capital city was (unsurprisingly) LON; it then became LAP ('London Air Port') and then LHR ('London Heathrow'). In the same way, Gatwick's code is LGW. New York's John F. Kennedy was initially called 'Idlewild', a somewhat dreamy and idyllic moniker that brought about the code IDL. After the new name was conferred, it became simply JFK. Amsterdam's designator is also simple (AMS), as is Frankfurt's (FRA).

However, not all airports have such easily deduced codes; some bear no relation to the letters of the city they serve. The capital of the United States has two airports. Its oldest, today known as 'Ronald Reagan National Airport', carries the designator 'DCA' to represent the city's full name of Washington, D.C. (as in D.C. Airport). However, its international airport code is 'IAD', which stands for International Airport Dulles. The 'Dulles' part refers to John Foster Dulles, the US Secretary of State under Republican President Dwight D. Eisenhower from 1953 to 1959.

Landside and Airside

You are landside when you get out of your car, bus, or train and enter the terminal, or when you have arrived and passed through immigration, picked up your bags, and (if you are an international passenger) gone through customs. Once you have gone through check-in and security, you are airside. The term 'airside' also refers to aircraft parking areas, taxiways, and runways.

Boeing Customer Numbers

The USA's Boeing Aircraft Company, now one of only two major airliner manufacturers in the world, assigns a number to each type of aircraft they build. Since the company's first jet airliner, the late 1950s-era Boeing 707, their aircraft have come in a variety of versions (or sub-types). For example, there is the Boeing 707-100, 707-200, 707-300, and 707-400. This numerical aircraft type and sub-type identification style has carried on with Boeing's airliners right through to the newest—the 787 Dreamliner.

The number after the aircraft type on the company's airliners denotes the sub-type, and the following number is the customer number. Therefore, a Boeing 707-436 is a -400 sub-type, with '36' being the customer number for British Airways and its international predecessor BOAC.

This customer number remains with the aircraft for its in-use lifetime, even if it is sold on and flies with a different airline. As an example, British Airways were one of the first two airlines to order the Boeing 757, the other being the long-since-defunct Eastern Airlines of Miami. BA used its 757-236s for over twenty years before selling them on, with most becoming cargo-carrying freighters for DHL. Even in DHL service, they are still Boeing 757-236 aircraft.

Call Signs

All airlines have their own unique call signs that preface flight numbers. Many airlines simply use their name or initials, but others are more creative. Pan American's nautical origins gave it the call sign 'Clipper', used also to prefix the names carried on all of the company's aircraft. British Airways is 'Speedbird', which has nothing to do with Concorde but instead refers to the name of the stylised logo that graced BOAC's aircraft (and, for a time, those of British Airways) until 1984–86, when a new colour scheme and branding was introduced. The logo can still be found today on the platforms of Hatton Cross Underground station.

CAT

CAT stands for Clear Air Turbulence, which means sudden and often unexpected in-flight bumping and bouncing as the aircraft flies through what is otherwise a beautiful day. Turbulence is usually associated with bad weather, but very severe CAT has been known, at least in days gone by, to shake an aircraft into its constituent parts.

COMBI

Some airliners can have flexible interiors (most notably the Boeing 747), with part of the cabin carrying people and the rest carrying cargo. The combination can be varied to give the airline the most profitable way of using the aircraft.

CTA

CTA stands for Central Terminal Area, which is the cluster of terminals in one central part of the airport's area. CTAs are found at Heathrow, New York, and several other airports.

Elevator

On an aircraft, this is the part of the tail wings that controls going up or down. They are also known as horizontal stabilisers.

Freedoms of the Air

Post-war international agreements defined five Freedoms of the Air. These are: the freedom to fly over a country without landing; the freedom to make a 'technical' landing to refuel or undertake repairs; the right to fly from one's own country to another; the right to fly from another country to one's own; and the right to fly between two foreign countries on a trip that ends or begins in one's own country.

Most airline traffic falls under third or fourth freedom rights, which is that between two countries carried by the airlines of those two countries.

Fifth Freedom rights are really rather interesting. The fifth freedom of the air allows, for example, Air India to sell tickets to and carry passengers between London Heathrow and New York and back the other way. These rights are not held by just any airline, but are subject to agreements between the countries concerned. In the case of Air India, the agreement is between the UK, the USA, and, obviously, India; it came about mostly due to the large numbers of Indians living in both the UK and the USA.

Fin

The tall bit at the back, on which airlines paint their logo. The fin is not merely decorative; it also helps keep the aircraft straight and level.

Gate

The waiting room and door leading outside or to the Airbridge, where you board your flight.

Holding and Stacking

Before entering a runway, aircraft will often have to wait at a yellow line across the taxiway that marks the runway holding point. Arriving aircraft also often have to wait while still in the air, being directed by air traffic controllers to fly around in circles in a stack, gradually descending as they wait for their turn to land.

Legacy Carriers and Low-Cost Carriers

Legacy carriers are long-established airlines such as British Airways, Delta, and numerous others. Usually, they were state-owned at one point. Today, many of these airlines are now privatised and compete not only with each other, but also with airlines like Easyjet and Ryanair (in the UK) and Southwest (in the USA). These airlines often charge lower fares, but they also provide a more basic service.

The London Underground

The 'LU', as it is occasionally known, is not a political movement. More usually called 'the tube', it's the subway system that is used by millions to get around London. Since December 1977 it has linked the centre of London and all points around the capital with Heathrow.

Phonetic Alphabet

The breezy and poetic alternative alphabet that uses words instead of letters to prevent confusion over the radio. It is also used by police, fire, and ambulance services along with other organisations that communicate via radio.

   Like your car, aircraft carry a registration or the equivalent of a licence plate. Using letters or numbers, the phonetic alphabet is always used to identify aircraft registrations. For example, UK-registered aircraft always start with the letter 'G', followed by four letters. G-BOAC was a British Airways Concorde. The 'BOAC' part was inherited by BA when its predecessor, the British Overseas Airways Corporation, initially ordered the supersonic airliner. However, in this case, the letters translated as 'Golf—Bravo Oscar Alpha Charlie'.

Ramp

The areas in front of terminals where aircraft park, also known as 'apron' and 'airside'. The Dutch call it the 'platform', and in Germany it's the '*Vorfeld*'.

Remote and Contact Stands

Aircraft park on hardstands, which are located on the ramp (or apron). Known more simply as 'stands,' they are given an identity like A3 or C14 depending on where they are found on the apron. A contact stand is one actually located at a terminal, with an airbridge serving it. A remote stand is used when the aircraft has to go somewhere else because there is no room at the terminal to park. In this situation, old-fashioned boarding stairs are used to get into and out of the remotely parked aircraft and buses are required to get passengers to and from the terminal itself.

SST

This stands for Super Sonic Transport, as in Concorde, the Soviet Union's Tupolev-designed equivalent, and the American version (which was mainly referred to as the Boeing SST, although this was inaccurate).

Taxiways and Runways

Runways are the very wide lengths of concrete or tarmac that aircraft take off and land on. Taxiways are the more slender airport roads used to get an aircraft to or from the runway to the ramp (or apron).

Threshold

The end of a runway—marked out with what looks like a pedestrian crossing, sometimes called 'piano keys', and the number of the runway heading.

Wet Lease and Dry Lease

If you are an airline and need an extra aircraft, either for a short period or a longer one, you can 'hire' one either under wet lease or dry lease terms. A wet lease means hiring only the aircraft itself, whereas a dry lease means taking the aircraft, the pilots to fly it, and the cabin crew to attend to the needs of the passengers. At one time, all airlines bought the aircraft they operated outright; today, few airlines do this, with most aircraft acquired on a long-term lease. With bigger airlines, this can often mean leasing an aircraft for the duration of its design life.

Wide Bodies and Narrow Bodies

In commercial aviation terms, 'wide bodied' and 'narrow bodied' refer to the width of various airliners. Examples of wide-bodied airliners include the Airbus A300, A310, A330, A340, A350, and especially the A380, in addition to the Boeing 747, 767, and 777. Although they are now retired from passenger service, the Douglas DC10 and Lockheed L1011 TriStar were also wide-bodied airliners. All of the above featured twin aisles in their cabins. Smaller aircraft have only one aisle, and they are referred to as narrow bodies. While in the air, large jets will add the word 'heavy' to their call sign and flight number to inform air traffic controllers that it is a large aircraft.

1
Approaching

I am who I am today because of the choices I made yesterday.

Eleanor Roosevelt

I am a passenger; I am not a pilot, or a member of any airline's cabin crew, or anything directly involved with aviation. This a description that applies to most people who travel by air. Some fly out of necessity, and others because it's the most practical way to get to where they want to go and come back again. Many are ambivalent about flying; some fly with a little concern, a few are utterly petrified of it, and some love it.

Whatever their view, if you were to ask anybody in the UK (or perhaps anywhere) to name an aircraft without thinking, there is a fair chance that the Spitfire would be mentioned. It was the iconic Royal Air Force (RAF) fighter that fought off Nazi Germany's aerial hordes in the Battle of Britain in 1940.

The Hurricane was actually used in greater numbers, but the Spitfire looked better—more graceful and more deadly, at least to the enemy. As it became apparent to the Germans that the fight for control of Britain's skies would not be won, the Luftwaffe's leader, Hermann Goering, asked his frontline commanders what more he could give them to help. One reply was: 'A squadron of Spitfires.'

A second well-known aircraft is Concorde, a third is the Boeing 747 Jumbo Jet, and a fourth is the (more recent) Airbus A380 double-decked 'Super-Jumbo'.

The era of mass air travel sees most flights—with big aircraft or small—depart and arrive more or less on time, and with your bags. They will also usually complete their journeys safely. However, very occasionally, things do go slightly amiss.

I have flown much less than some, but more than others. Although I have never missed a flight (I did come close once with a flight from Heathrow to New York, but I made it), like a few, I have been upgraded, downgraded, and have had my baggage go somewhere else. I have bounced through storms and bounced just as much in clear air. I have been strapped into my seat, watching as my airline dinner rose in the air as the aircraft plummeted through an air pocket. I have even enjoyed my airline meal enough to ask if I could have another one, and I got it, too—a smile from the USA's United Airlines, whose advertising tag was 'Fly the Friendly Skies' some years ago. I have been quizzed by immigration officials and quizzed again by customs officials, though only once. I have

The two towers. The 1955 tower is in the foreground, with its successor in the background. (*Simon Boddy*)

mostly flown smoothly. I have also been a 'stand-by' passenger, hoping for a spare seat (which I did get), and I have been 'bumped'.

'Bumped' seems to have a singular appropriateness when applied to the airline industry. It is the term used when an airline overbooks a flight and everybody actually turns up. Airlines take a calculated gamble with bookings; on most flights, there are more passengers booked than the aircraft has seats for, but the number of no-shows can be astoundingly high. No-shows cost the airline equally astoundingly large amounts of money, so they almost always overbook flights. This practice usually works, but on rare occasions everybody actually arrives at the terminal wanting to fly—so people get bumped.

Like everybody else, I have been patted down, searched, and x-rayed, and in modern times I have had to look at facial-recognition cameras. I have been asked if I packed my bags myself. I have waited for a delayed flight and departed on an on-time flight, and I have arrived on time too. I have arrived late, rushing through an airport's sprawling miasma of signs, inter-terminal trains, up escalators and down, bypassing hordes of others all doing the same, to make a connecting flight. I have flown by day and by night, long-haul and short-haul.

Whatever the experience, I am an enthusiast, an aviation geek, and a journalist, sometimes handy with a camera. I write about aviation (amongst other things), and I point my camera in the general direction of whatever it is I want to photograph, use auto-focus, hope, and luck, and see what it looks like later. I am not, however, an aviation professional. I dabble in other subjects, but I like commercial airliners and airlines. And I like airports—especially airports.

I am one of the few who does not care if my flight is delayed. Delays happen; they mean being stuck at an airport somewhere, so I'm not unhappy about them. In my very early childhood, my father (Forces broadcaster Terry James) and I went from London Heathrow to New York on a brand-new Vickers Super VC10 for a month-long trip around the USA on a Greyhound bus. The return trip was delayed due to a technical problem with the aircraft, an American-built Boeing 707-436 powered by Rolls-Royce Engines—one of which caused the delay.

BOAC re-booked every passenger on other flights back to Heathrow—except for me and my dad. We weren't in a hurry and I was at an airport, so I was happy. We also had a very attentive cabin crew all the way back across the Atlantic. A Boeing 707 is very roomy when you are one of only two passengers on board.

The same cannot be said for John F. Kennedy (JFK) International Airport, New York. It is a cramped and crowded place when busy, just like its cousin across the ocean in London. New York's JFK and London's Heathrow share a number of common traits. Both were born in the whirlwind conflict of the Second World War. Both started life as multi-runway fields, with both losing some of those runways as expanding aircraft parking areas meant the space was needed. Both have been rebuilt extensively in recent years to handle traffic loads that were never part of their original design. Both are, of themselves, the commercial aviation equivalent of twenty-four-hour cities that teem with life every day throughout the year. London to New York and *vice versa* is considered by some to be the Blue Riband of air travel, to the point where Concorde was used more extensively between the two cities than on any other route (the other prime route for Concorde was from Paris to New York, but British Airways ran more services from London than Air France ever did).

While the similarities between the two airports can be quite striking, the difference is that Heathrow handles more international traffic than JFK by some distance. Heathrow held the title of the world's busiest international airport almost from the day it opened, only being pushed back in more recent years by fast-growing airports like Dubai, where the gigantic new Dubai World Central Airport has been built and traffic rockets ever-upwards by the thrusting and continually expanding Emirates Airlines, who have more Airbus A380 'Super Jumbo' aircraft than anybody else. Unfortunately, open desert is a little hard to find in the green fields of southern England, just as it is in New York.

Space to build big new airports (or to expand existing ones) has always been hard to find, and apart from the deserts of the Middle East, there have been only two truly large new airports built since the Boeing 747 went into service in 1969—Dallas/Fort Worth, Texas, and Denver, Colorado, in the United States. However, both have US domestic traffic as their primary business—unlike Heathrow or, for that matter, Dubai, where most of the traffic comes from other countries.

London's status as the centre of the planet is today under threat from other cities that demand their place at the top table of world affairs, like the intentionally and aggressively named Dubai World Central. London's importance was initially gained as a result of its docks, now a shadow of their once-glorious heyday. Since the late 1970s, London's importance has been maintained by Heathrow Airport.

By any measurement, Heathrow remains one of the world's greatest airports. However, most people neither know nor care. Most people are passengers—like me. They simply want to go from one place to another, preferably quickly and definitely safely. How many runways Heathrow had, has, or will have is of no concern to them. All are often crammed into a long, thin aluminium tube full of others with the same desire, and to many, that long, thin aluminium tube is pretty much the same as any other—regardless of the colours painted on the outside.

As the aircraft descends towards Heathrow, some might take a look out the window and see what can be seen. The view of central London can be spectacular—at least, it is if you have a window seat on the right-hand side of the aircraft as it sinks gracefully over the city towards runway 25 left or right, approaching from the east. The same sights have been seen since January 1946—Aldwych, The Strand and the Central Law Courts, the Houses of Parliament and Big Ben, Victoria Railway Station, Buckingham Palace and Brentford Football Club. If your interest in football doesn't cover the less-fashionable teams, Chelsea's Stamford Bridge Arena is also easily seen. However, due to Brentford's position not far from the runway's end, for many years the stadium roof was painted with a white message on a blue background—'Next time, fly KLM'.

There are still some areas around Heathrow that seem very underdeveloped. (*Author*)

Local residents. (*Author*)

The Green Man pub and a Royal Jordanian Airlines Boeing 787. (*Author*)

THE GREEN MAN

Originally constructed in the 16th Century, parts of the building date back to circa 1640.

The Green Man pub has a long tradition of local hostelry, serving many a weary traveller on their way to and from London.

Many historical legends also surround the pub including the ghost of The Grey Lady and Highwaymen, reportedly to include the infamous Dick Turpin who hid in the secret chamber behind the fireplace.

Help us to keep up the colourful history of The Green Man pub, come in and let us take care of you.

History. (*Author*)

There have been one or two additions to London since 1946 (the London Eye being one of the most prominent), but the landmarks there in 1946 are still there now, today, seventy years after the first aircraft arrived at Heathrow.

Another of these landmarks is the Green Man public house. It can be found right under the final approach to runway 27 left. By that point, the landing gear is down, flaps are set for landing, and everybody, including the cabin crew, will be strapped in for touchdown. To get a glimpse of The Green Man, you still need to be sitting on the right of the aircraft. However, you'll need to be quick, as it's almost but not quite directly under your landing airliner, so it's easy to miss as you speed by. If the legend of Dick Turpin is true, the pub is also where he hid while on the run from the law, in a concealed cubby-hole behind the fireplace. The cubby-hole does exist, even if Turpin himself never used it.

If you sit on the left side of the aircraft, you might get a quick glance at what appears to be a riot—smoke, flames, and people trying to damage each other. Some of those people wear uniforms, carrying shields and batons as they avoid a brick being thrown at them. This is the Metropolitan Police Training School, but you have to be quick to spot it as your flight swoops towards the Great West Road and Heathrow's two runways, as equally eagle-eyed as one needs to be to spot the Green Man.

You don't get to see much of central London if you sit on the left. Sit on the right; it's more revealing (as long as it's not cloudy).

If arriving aircraft approach from the west, landings are usually on runway 09 left. The flight path takes one directly over Windsor, and the castle can be glimpsed, briefly, just to the left of the descending aircraft.

For sale, with room for one Airbus A380. The village of Longford, just north of the threshold of runway 09 left, is doomed to be buried under the concrete of the new third runway and aircraft parking. Most of the houses in Longford were bought by a hotel chain and are used to house immigrants (temporarily or otherwise). (*Author*)

If they are not peering out of their window, the average passenger will be gripping the armrests of their seat, hoping that their landing is smooth and that they can get off quickly, picking up their bags, getting through the terminal, and going about their business. The only interaction with those who are there to help them along are mere faces, seen only briefly as they ask how to get into London. They are passengers; they have arrived.

2
Beginning

Thus things proceed in their circle and thus the Empire is maintained.

Machiavelli

Numerous books and magazine articles have been written about the history of Heathrow Airport—some accurate, and some marginally less so—but history never stops being made. Nevertheless, one can justifiably ask how many ways there are to tell an already well-told story, but perhaps there are some who are unaware of Heathrow's early days and what lay there before the airport spread its way over the 1,226 hectares it now occupies. In truth, there was not very much to be found; a map from 1754 shows a narrow lane winding its way south from the London to Bath Road until it met the southwest road from Brentford to Staines. It was named Cain's Lane, and halfway along it a second lane ran east, with a small hamlet of houses on the northern side, facing Hounslow Heath as it spread its way southward. By 1914, much of the area was agricultural land.

The airport's story starts with Richard Fairey. Many sites now occupied by airports previously contained airfields; the area now taken up by New York's JFK International Airport originally held a flying field and a golf course. Hounslow Heath's row of houses were almost directly opposite Richard Fairey's airfield.

An enterprising and ambitious young man, Fairey was twenty-eight when he started his own aircraft manufacturing company. His timing was advantageous; it was 1915, and war was blighting Europe. Fairey started off in a small factory in Hayes, but by 1929 he had established the Fairey Aircraft Company as one of Britain's foremost aviation businesses. Fairey had been using RAF Northolt to test aircraft, but sharing anything with the military is always problematic. The military mind-set is by nature an enquiring one, and sometimes it is just plain nosy—especially when there is a war on. This led Fairey to find a new site, 4 miles south of Hayes. The land was flat and open, there was no urban sprawl, and the biggest advantage was the Great South West Road, which had opened just three years earlier, only a mile south along Cain's Lane. The new road provided quick access to both London and Fairey's seaplane testing base on the south coast.

Fairey purchased 150 acres of land from the Vicar of Harmondsworth, with additional plots also acquired to create Fairey's new airfield. Shaped like a 'V', with the point facing south (or a drunken 'L' leaning a bit to the left), the airfield was known by several different names. Most often, it was known by those who used it as the 'Fairey Aerodrome'; sometimes it was the 'Great West Aerodrome', and occasionally it was called by the name of the tiny village that lay just to the north of it—Heath Row.

However, it was never the 'original' Heathrow Airport because it was never an airport at all—merely a test airfield. It is not a hard mistake to make; in the Second World War, even the German Luftwaffe identified the Fairey Aerodrome on their maps by using the name commonly used for the hamlet over the road. Ever since then, the Fairey Aerodrome has been persistently and erroneously called 'Heathrow' (prior to the Second World War, London's air transport needs were catered for at Croydon). While Richard Fairey's airfield was used only for test flights, it had a hangar in the north-east corner that was the largest of its type in the world. It also had a concrete apron and, like most airfields, grass take-off and landing areas.

The first hint of further development of the area was felt in 1935 with the building of sewage works at Perry Oaks, not far to the west of the airfield, but such fripperies were of no concern to the powerful and influential people who attended the first Royal Aeronautical Society garden party at the aerodrome. The first event was considered to be so successful that it was held annually from then on. The occasion was always exclusive and closed to the general public. As another war loomed across Europe in 1939, only twenty-one years after the first had come to an end, the Society held its last event before the conflict began. Among those present was the government's Under-Secretary of State for Air, Harold Balfour. Like most, Balfour was preoccupied with the potential war; the German invasion of Poland was only weeks away. However, he was also considering the state of civil air transport in Britain, and the Fairey Aerodrome would play a key role in this within a few years.

Balfour had been a pilot in the First World War, and on occasion he had exhibited an un-British ruthlessness when dealing with the enemy. He combined politics with championing civil aviation; he had been keen on Heston, a few miles to the north-east of the Fairey airfield, being expanded and redeveloped as London's airport since Croydon had already become too small, and the Heston Extension Act became the last bill to be passed in parliament before war broke out.

War tends to focus minds on the advancement and development of existing weaponry and infrastructure in order to beat the enemy. At the road research laboratory on the Bath Road, near Harmondsworth and not far from both Heston and Fairey's test airfield, Professor Barnes Wallis worked on his bouncing bomb. Hard-surface runways were another development; with bomber and transport aircraft getting bigger and heavier, grass runways were no longer practicable. With the most suitable airfields being some distance from London, Balfour realised that even an expanded Heston would be too small as far as commercial air transport was concerned. As he held the responsibility for civil aviation in addition to his wartime duties, he took the odd moment to consider what would be needed for the capital city once the war was over. He spent a part of his spare time minutely examining a large-scale map of London and the surrounding countryside, using a celluloid grid to illustrate the area that might be required for a big new airport. He found just one site that ticked all the boxes; Richard Fairey's airfield and the land that surrounded it, including the hamlet of Heath Row.

In 1943 he set out his thoughts in a note to his own under-secretary, Sir Arthur Street, with four main points:

1. Heston is now too small to accommodate both current and future needs.
2. The possibilities of a site at Heath Row [*sic.*] should be fully explored with a view to meeting both current and future requirements.
3. Britain will require at least three air ports capable of handling trans oceanic aircraft; London, Liverpool and Prestwick. It is unlikely all three will be fogbound at the same time.
4. We cannot build now due to war-time shortages of both men and materials. Furthermore, if we build now, and the war continues, there will be further rapid advances in aviation and our work will quickly become as out of date as our Heston scheme now appears.

With the war in Europe beginning to go the way of the Allies and the defeat of Germany thus considered to be a matter of time, attention turned to defeating Japan. This gave Balfour the chance to indulge in some slightly underhanded methods of getting the airfield he believed was going to be needed.

Balfour presented a proposal document to the government, arguing that a large, new air base close to London was needed to allow the RAF to transport men and supplies to the Far East. Balfour knew perfectly well that there were already airfields in the south east that were capable of handling such an operation, but he believed that the economic benefits of a specifically civil-use airfield were strong enough for the case to be made.

He made his point emphatically well, winning the debate. Using emergency wartime powers, the Air Ministry requisitioned the land required. The sleepy little collection of houses by the heath were flattened. To the undeniably justified fury of Richard Fairey, who was conveniently out of the way in Washington at the time, his aerodrome was also included in the plan. Fairey had to move to Heston and share it with the RAF; it has been said that the disruption caused by this enforced move contributed to the eventual decline of Fairey's company. It is not clear what the former residents of Heathrow made of being forced to leave their homes, but they did, at least, get better houses out of it—many of the ones they had left had no running water or electricity.

While Balfour's manoeuvring was convincing everybody that the new airfield would be an RAF base, the area's possibilities had been spotted, seemingly independently, by Brigadier-General Alfred Critchley, Director-General of the British Overseas Airways Corporation (BOAC). BOAC had been formed in April 1940 and operated wartime services under the control of the Air Ministry.

Critchley found it irksome that the company had to operate from Whitchurch, 120 miles from the capital of the country it had been established to serve, particularly since the airline's headquarters were in central London. Critchley lived at Sunningdale, and his daily journey to work took him along the Great South West Road and past the flat expanse of what was becoming, supposedly, a military airfield. Apparently putting two and two together, Critchley made a point of stopping each day and walking around the area; at one point, he invited then-Secretary of State for Air Sir Archibald Sinclair's under-secretary to join him. It is unclear whether the under-secretary revealed that Harold Balfour already had the matter in hand, and Critchley never let on either; however, he later called a press conference and announced that a new home for Britain's national airline was to be built only 12.5 miles from Hyde Park Corner, Central London. Critchley remarked:

> It will cover 2,800 acres, be larger than New York's new airport at Idlewild and have a runway 5,000 yards long and 300 yards wide, with a water runway for flying boats 4,000 yards long and 200 yards wide. I can tell you about it—but I can't tell you where it is yet.

His motives for this somewhat-misleading statement remain unclear, with no clues offered in his 1960 biography. Perhaps he wanted to increase his stature, representing himself as the founder of Heathrow Airport despite that title actually belonging to Harold Balfour. Perhaps he simply wanted to hurry things along, pressuring the government to transfer use of the airfield from the RAF to civilian operations, thus giving his airline the London base it needed. Whatever Critchley's reasons, three months later, in June 1944, *The Daily Telegraph* ran a story that offered unofficial (and in some cases very exaggerated) details of what was to be built west of London. The story repeated Critchley's claims of a 5-mile runway and stated that the airport would be the biggest in the world, which must have been something of a surprise to those who thought that Heathrow was going to be an RAF base.

None of the runways would reach the absurd 5-mile length suggested by Critchley and the article. However, by the standards of the time, the work that went into building the site was huge. Three concrete runways were built in the standard RAF triangle, each one measuring 300 feet wide. They were built to handle any aircraft then in existence (and remarkably, they have been able to handle all built since). The northern runway, still in use today, was built over the remains of Caesar's camp and the end of Roy's baseline, necessitating the removal of the famous cannon.

Harold Balfour's involvement in the project came to an end with the creation of the Ministry for Civil Aviation; Prime Minister Winston Churchill chose to place Lord Swinton as head of the organisation, and Balfour departed to become Resident Minister in West Africa.

Two days after Germany's surrender brought the war in Europe to an end, Lord Swinton chaired a meeting between ministry officials and airline chiefs to formulate a short-term policy for London Airports. The government had decided that Heathrow should become the principal airport for London; however, due to construction work currently underway, the airport would not be available for some time. Before any firm decisions could be made, the May 1945 general election saw the Winston Churchill-led coalition replaced by a Labour government, with Lord Winster taking over from Lord Swinton as Minister for Civil Aviation. A further meeting provided a solution to the country's short-term aviation needs by using Northolt —despite objections from the RAF, whose airfield it was—with long-distance flights operating from Hurn, near Bournemouth.

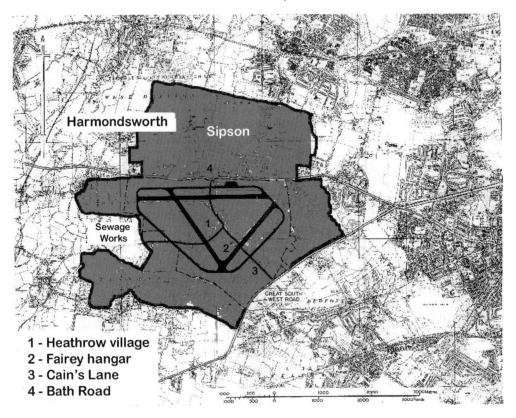

The land requisitioned for the airport, as shown in 1945. (*Author's collection*)

After the surrender of Japan and the end of the Second World War, RAF Heathrow was left with no credible role to fill. Nevertheless, the construction work continued. Within weeks of Japan's surrender, the Ministry of Civil Aviation appointed a panel of experts to consider how best to adapt the site's triangular layout for civil use. The panel's title was 'The London Airport Advisory Layout Panel'—the first official incidence of the new airfield being referred to as 'London Airport'.

Air Vice-Marshal Donald Bennett, an Australian, had numerous achievements to his name. Perhaps the most well-known example of these was his status as the founder of the Pathfinder Force, whose wartime role was to mark targets for bombers. With the war over, Bennett left the RAF to head a new airline being formed by a consortium of shipping companies. The consortium's airline was to be named British South American Airways (BSAA). As the airline's chief, Bennett attended the meetings held to decide the immediate future of air services to and from London. With BOAC and the US airlines laying claim to the limited space available at Hurn, and Northolt being used for shorter European-focussed services, BSAA were going to have a problem getting started at all. However, Bennett was extremely resourceful, as he had showed so many times in the war—in addition to his other achievements, he had risen to become the RAF's youngest Air Vice-Marshal—and he requested that his airline be allowed to use the new airport at Heathrow since one of the runways was already complete.

Lord Winster was now proving to be something of a supporter of both commercial aviation and the new airport, so a deal was quickly agreed—even though there were still no permanent terminal facilities ready and the flights were to be described as 'route-proving'. On the same day as BSAA's first flight, control of the airfield would pass from the military to the Ministry of Civil Aviation. The date set for the transfer of control and the start of BSAA's flights was 1 January 1946.

The best aircraft immediately available for BSAA's first service was a converted Avro Lancaster bomber. Although not ideal for use in civil service, the Manchester-built aircraft had proved itself to be a useful type during the war; it had successfully delivered the bouncing bomb, which had been developed just along the Bath Road from where Heathrow's first departure was about to take place. Don Bennett himself flew the aircraft to the new airport; the converted Lancaster was dubbed *The Lancastrian* by its manufacturer, while BSAA named it *Starlight*. It seemed apt that a converted warplane should be the first to take off from a partially built airfield whose reason for being was rooted in conflict.

Lord Winster made the most of the occasion, with a busload of press and dignitaries being given a tour of what was still very much a work in progress. In his speech, Winster declared that the new airport would allow Britain to assume its rightful place on the world stage. Shortly afterwards, at 12.05 p.m., *Starlight* took off with ten passengers and 5,000 lbs of mail on board.

As air services rapidly developed, other airlines continued to use Hurn, near Bournemouth. They were not at all happy that their passengers had to make an almost 100-mile coach journey to actually reach the city they were heading to, particularly with the last leg of that trip taking them along the Great West Road, from where they could see the new airport taking shape. Lord Winster had intended to at least keep the big operators away from Heathrow until the first triangle of runways and a permanent terminal had been finished. However, with other airlines demanding to follow BSAA's lead, not long after the departure of *Starlight*, he announced that the new airport would officially open just over four months later—despite the fact that there was still no terminal. This concern was overridden by the airlines still using Hurn, all of whom required the use of an airport closer to London.

BOAC began operating from Heathrow a few days before the official opening, when a Lancastrian departed for Australia. On opening day itself, the first arrival was another of BOAC's Lancastrians making the reverse journey, arriving from Sydney after a sixty-three-hour trip. By noon, Pan American and American Overseas Airlines had a pair of new Lockheed Constellations on the ramp. The ultra-modern lines of the US-built aircraft, designed specifically for air transport, contrasted sharply with the more functional shape and war-time origins of the British Lancastrian - while Britain's pioneering contributions to aviation are undeniable, the sad fact remains that for one reason or another, the country has either lagged behind its competitors or thrown away its leading position and has done so for decades.

Even though the Americans had been made aware of the lack of facilities, they were still surprised to note that not only did their aircraft appear more modern than their British counterparts, but so did their terminals. The Americans had departed from

A Trans Canada Lockheed Constellation in the 1940s. (*Colin Dodds collection*)

A Qantas Lockheed Constellation in the 1940s. (*Colin Dodds collection*)

Into the 1950s; a BOAC Douglas DC7. (*Colin Dodds collection*)

relatively comfortable and newly built structures (even though they were only interim buildings), arriving to find tents, caravans, and a row of red telephone boxes. The weather that summer was not helpful, and duckboards were placed outside the tents to keep the passengers' feet clear of the mud and prevent them from tripping over the ropes holding the tents up. The canvas collection of temporary facilities lay on the north side of the airfield, tightly crammed in between the Bath Road and the as-yet only fully constructed runway—Runway No. 1. The sign at the airport's entrance read: 'London Airport, Heath Row'—a throwback, perhaps, to the row of houses that once faced the heath.

As Winster had promised, London's new airport officially opened on May 31 1946. By September, the RAF's triangle of runways was complete.

With the approaching nationalisation of British airlines, BSAA came under the control of the British Overseas Airways Corporation. The Civil Aviation Act 1946 set up the three-nationally owned air carriers, with BSAA becoming a government-owned corporation on 1 August of that year. It was given the responsibility of developing services from the UK to South America. The airline's network was further expanded later in 1946, covering routes to the West Indies and Central America.

In January 1947, fifteen months after it had been established, the London Airport Advisory Layout Panel presented its report. The panel's brief had been to examine the best way of developing the still-new site into a major civil airport while maintaining as much of the completed work as possible—including the three runways, which had been designed primarily for the RAF's needs. The new requirements were for a 7-square-mile site, including an area north of the Bath Road. This area had been earmarked for future development, but it would mean the destruction of the village of Sipson; given the post-war housing shortage, the government were reluctant to pursue this course at the time.

The residents of Sipson have been living with this threat ever since, and, as of 2016, there is still a housing shortage.

The panel's report was brief and to the point, recommending the retention of two of the existing runways—No. 1, the first to be completed and running parallel with the Bath Road, and No. 2, the most easterly of the three. The panel also recommended that Runway No. 3, the most westerly, be moved half a mile further west, thus making the triangle larger. A second triangle was then to be built, resulting in a 'Star of David' layout with the terminal and control tower being constructed in the centre and reached by a road tunnel that ran under the northern runway.

This phase of development was referred to as 'Stage 2', with 'Stage 1'—the original, smaller RAF triangle—already completed. 'Stage 3' was to be the building of the third triangle of runways north of the Bath Road; the road itself would be diverted around the site. The plans also included provisions to extend the runways further when the need arose.

Had that extra triangle been built, the significant furore over the proposals for building what is known as Heathrow's 'third' runway would not have arisen seventy years later. Heathrow would have started life with nine runways, and even though some of those would have been taken out of use and concreted over to provide additional aircraft parking and terminal extensions (as they have been), the airport would have the runway capacity it needs today. In fact, Heathrow actually had three runways right up

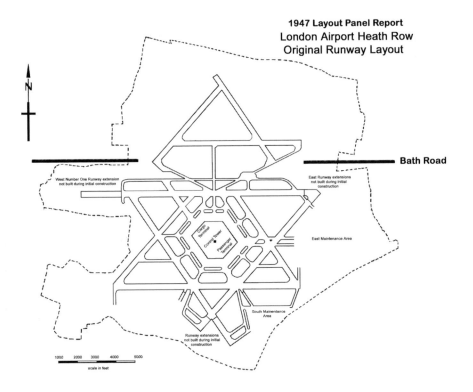

The Layout Panel's initial plan in 1947. (*Author's collection*)

until work commenced on building the newest terminal; Runway No. 2 had been in use for most of the airport's history.

For those unfamiliar with the numbering of the runways, some explanation will be needed. In the original layout, the panel numbered the runways '1', '2', and '3'—referring to the three built for what was supposed to be an RAF airfield. Runway No. 3 was not retained, of course, but rather than keep the number, its replacement became Runway No. 4. The second triangle of runways—Stage 2—were numbered '5', '6', and '7'. Had Stage 3 gone ahead, the trio of runways north of the Bath Road would have been numbered '8', '9', and '10'.

Just to confuse matters a little more, aircrews and controllers use a different method of identifying runways. This is based on a compass bearing, giving two designators for a single runway—one at each end. Heathrow's first runway, running alongside the Bath Road, is close to a heading of 94 degrees when approached from the west and 274 when approached from the east (over London itself). The final digit of these numbers is rounded up or down to the nearest ten—90 and 270 respectively—and the zero is then removed, resulting in '9' and '27'. When a runway consists of a parallel pair, it is necessary to specify which side is which; therefore, when approaching from the west, the runways become '9 Left' and '9 Right', and if approaching from the east, they become '27 Left' and '27 Right'.

The end of each runway is marked with a broad series of black and white strips that looks more like a pedestrian crossing than a runway. The ensemble is then topped by the runway's compass designation.

In addition to the layout panel's report being delivered, 1947 saw the appointment of the airport's first general manager (or 'Aerodrome Commandant', as they were called at the time). Air Marshal Sir John Henry D'Albiac KCVO KBE CB DSO was, as his titles suggest, a man with a distinguished service record. Although he was a highly likeable person, he tended to want to get things done in the manner of the armed forces, which did not always meet with the appreciation of the airlines. Nevertheless, he is generally recognised as being a fine man who did a lot to help get things moving while the airport was still being built.

As the work had gone on, the entire area had changed beyond recognition. Old roads such as Cain's Lane—which led north from the Great Southwest Road to the Bath Road, and provided access to the Fairey Airfield—now came to a sudden halt just a few feet from where they began, with the new perimeter blocking their previous paths.

The introduction of the Boeing Stratocruiser—the last word in in-flight luxury—spelled the end for seaplanes as the primary means of air travel. Almost inevitably, the first Stratocruiser was delivered to Pan American, who, along with BOAC, had pioneered long-distance seaplane use. The aircraft first arrived at Heathrow in June 1949, the same month that BOAC absorbed BSAA. BOAC's own 'Strats' (as the new aircraft were often called) entered service at the end of the year, by which time the facilities on the Bath Road were fit to burst—a sign of things to come.

Although the tents and duckboards had been replaced by more solid buildings, they were still far too small to cope with the growing passenger numbers. The same was true with the apron, which was almost always full to the point of overflowing; in between flights, increasing numbers of aircraft had to be parked on Runway No. 3.

The airport begins to take shape in the 1950s. (*Author's collection*)

Adding to the ballooning number of passengers being stuffed into the airport, BOAC's shorter routes had been transferred to the second state-owned airline, British European Airlines (BEA). BEA's services had initially run from RAF Northolt, situated a few miles north of the new airport, but were moved to Heathrow as the RAF wanted Northolt to return to exclusive military use by 1954.

With the passing of the Air Corporations Act 1949, the British South American Airways Corporation became the South American Division of BOAC, with the change becoming effective from 1 January 1950. The strain that the new airport was under became even more noticeable in 1950, when Runway No. 1—the closest to the Bath Road terminal—was closed to allow the digging of a giant ditch across it. With Runway No. 5 now open at the far side of the airfield, aircraft had to taxi for a long time when departing or arriving. However, the ditch was at least a tangible sign that relief was not too far away. The closure of Runway No. 1 was to allow the building of the 2,080-foot-long tunnel into the central area. It would have four lanes for road traffic and a pedestrian walkway, linking the new terminal (in the centre of the Star of David runway pattern) with the outside world.

On 1 February 1952, King George VI and the Queen came to the airport to wave farewell to their daughter, Princess Elizabeth, and the Duke of Edinburgh, who were departing for a five-month tour of the Commonwealth. The aircraft departed at 12.11 p.m. from the distant Runway No. 5; as the King watched, his view was somewhat obscured by the building work going on in the central area. It was the last time

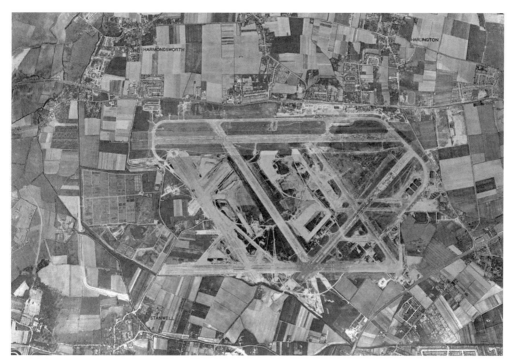

The Central Area becomes apparent. Cain's Lane can still be seen, but there is no trace of the houses that once stood in the middle of the site. (*Author's collection*)

The tunnel and Central Area are identifiable in 1954. (*Author's collection*)

Princess Elizabeth would see her father—he died a week later. Departing as a princess, Elizabeth returned to Heathrow on 7 February as Queen.

To a large extent, post-war commercial aviation had been dominated by the US manufacturers Boeing and Douglas, albeit with a significant contribution by Lockheed's Constellation. However, it was Britain who took the lead on the last day of 1951, when BOAC took delivery of its first De Havilland Comet 1 Jetliner.

With the arrival of the jet engine, two things immediately became apparent. The first was that the blast from the aircraft's engines was powerful enough to cause considerable damage to anything behind it, so blast-proof fences were needed to protect buildings. The second was noise; jet engines were an entirely different proposition for those living near the airport or under the flight path, and the plan for the third triangle of runways (north of the Bath Road) came under increasing scrutiny. Residents in the village of Sipson were particularly concerned because their village was expected to be demolished completely, along with parts of Harlington.

In December 1952, in response to a question from Uxbridge MP Frank Beswick, Alan Lennox-Boyd, the then-Minister of Civil Aviation, announced that the third triangle would not be built:

> Careful analysis of the results of a programme of practical experiments recently concluded by my department have shown that the additional amount of traffic which could be accepted by extending the airport north of the Bath Road would not justify the expenditure and disturbance caused by the extension.

In other words, the third triangle would cost too much, and no politician wanted to risk losing votes over expanding an already large and noisy airport.

In 1954, the Royal Aeronautical Society held another garden party at what was left of the Fairey Aerodrome. Now situated in the middle of a massive building site, the changes to the scenery did at least allow a Boeing Stratocruiser, a Lockheed Constellation, and a brand new Vickers Viscount—Britain's latest short-haul turbo-prop airliner—to be parked close by for inspection.

The weather was as unkind as ever, and, given the nature of what had overtaken Richard Fairey's test airfield, it seemed a little incongruous to be staging a garden party while aircraft from the world's airlines were also arriving and departing. It was the first Society garden party held since before the war, and it was also the last.

A few days later, on the thirty-fifth anniversary of Alcock and Brown's pioneering first non-stop flight across the Atlantic, the Minister for Transport and Civil Aviation unveiled a statue of the two men next to the terminal buildings on the Bath Road. The statue was subsequently moved to the central area, and today it stands back on the north side of the airport—this time outside the Heathrow Academy on the Bath Road, not far from its original location.

The statue of Alcock and Brown is unveiled on the north side in 1954. (*Colin Dodds collection*)

3
Centrality

The airport runway is the most important main street in any town.

Norm Crabtree, former aviation director for the US state of Ohio

The central area was complete enough to use by April 1955, dominated by the 120-foot-tall control tower. This was later than originally planned, with cuts in government expenditure and industrial disputes (including strikes) contributing to the delay. From the control tower's viewing cab, perched on top of the brick-built structure, the controllers had a commanding view of the entire field of the now nearly complete airport.

Facing south, to the left of the front of the tower, on the south-east face of the diamond formed by the Star of David runway layout, was the long-awaited terminal. Designed by Sir Frederick Gibberd, the initial intention was for it to be used by shorter-range services. Long-haul flights would continue to use the Bath Road terminal, enabling BEA to move in from the start. Although it had already been in use for eight months, the terminal was officially opened by Queen Elizabeth on December 16; it was named the 'Europa Building'.

The third major building in the central area, next to the Europa Building, was also opened by Her Majesty; it was named 'The Queen's Building'. This was the airport's administrative nerve centre. The building featured roof gardens that extended onto the roof of the terminal next door, and a multi-deck observation gallery allowed people a close-up view of aircraft parked on the airside apron in front.

The continual growth in passenger figures and aircraft movements was already giving rise to concern over how the central area was to be developed. Under the chairmanship of Sir Eric Millbourn, a committee produced a report with a number of recommendations in August 1957. First and foremost, the report suggested expanding Gatwick Airport (to the south of London) to take the pressure off Heathrow. Secondly, the committee endorsed the layout proposal of having all passenger facilities located in the central area, suggesting the immediate construction of a long-haul terminal on the south-west face of the diamond (to the right of the control tower) and a new terminal just for BEA on the north-east face of the diamond, on the other side of the Queen's Building. A cargo terminal would be constructed on the fourth side of the diamond.

The control tower. (*David Winyard collection*)

'*No se puede confundir*'; White Horse whisky advertising in at least three languages.
(*David Winyard collection*)

The Europa Building. It has carried at least two names on the frontage—'No. 1 Passenger Building', as seen here, and then, once the jet era had begun, 'No. 1 Europa'. The building only lost its 'Europa' title when T1 was opened. (*David Winyard collection*)

As the name says… (*David Winyard collection*)

The committee also recommended use of the finger-and-gate system for passengers, with aircraft parked nose-in to the gates along each finger (or pier), since more aircraft could be accommodated in this way.

All this building work would clearly present something of a problem in the limited space of the central area, so the committee suggested (somewhat reluctantly) that two of the six runways (Nos 4 and 6, aligned in the north-west-to-south-east direction) should be closed. They reasoned that these runways had seen little use—especially Runway No. 6, the most easterly of the pair, which had already been used for additional aircraft parking.

Even this early in the airport's history, the limits imposed by having the terminal area lassoed by runways had become apparent. The central area had been in use for less than two and a half years. The same constraint was encountered at JFK, New York; it had started life with a central terminal area and seven runways, but two of them were never commissioned for use. The space was needed to park aircraft.

Curiously, the Fairey hangar remained in place until well into the jet age. It was initially used as the airport fire station, and for a while it was used to advertise BOAC's services as it stood on the other side of the apron and almost opposite the Europa Building.

Sir Frederick Gibberd was again called upon to design the new terminal, and he produced a larger version of his earlier design. This time he used more glass and less brick, giving the building a lighter and more airy feel. Its precise position somewhat altered the symmetry of the central area diamond because it was built further west, allowing for more car parking in front. The terminal was named the 'Oceanic Building', and BOAC moved across from the Bath Road site in November 1961, bringing their upgraded Comet 4 airliners and the new Boeing 707s with them. The Comet 4 had replaced the ill-fated Comet 1, and in 1958 it had narrowly beaten the US-built Boeing 707 into regular service. To celebrate the resumption of jet-airliner-operated schedules, one Comet departed from Heathrow to New York, with another simultaneously beginning its journey in the opposite direction. Pan American brought the 707 into use almost three weeks later, the first flight departing from JFK and heading to Paris.

By March 1962, all airlines were operating from either the Europa Building (serving UK domestic flights and, as the name implied, services to continental Europe) or the Oceanic Building (serving long-haul flights). For the first time, fifteen years since the layout panel had originally proposed it, all passenger journeys began or ended in the central area. With the opening of the M4 motorway in 1965, the vision of the airport's planners was now a reality. It was also the first time that the airport had been officially acknowledged as 'London Heathrow Airport'. A road journey that began in London took the departing passenger along a wide, modern highway until they reached the tunnel entrance, above which was an imposing sign that read 'Welcome to Heathrow'.

One did not simply drive through the tunnel—one swooped through it. Even the BEA buses that ran from London still swooped into the artificially-lit confines of this long, concrete-lined tube. BEA occupied the West London Air Terminal, which (as its name suggested) was in West London, on Cromwell Road. Passengers could check in for their flights at this building before boarding the airline's own buses for the ride to the airport. Their luggage was stowed in a trailer that was hooked to the rear of the bus, and its

One of Eagle Airways' US-built Douglas aircraft and a BEA Vanguard in 1960—with the two airlines going head-to-head in Europe. Richard Fairey's hangar still stands, advertising BOAC's cheap fares, right in front of the roof gardens. The promotions were a direct result of Eagle competing at Heathrow with the state-owned airlines. (*David Winyard collection*)

The finishing touches being made to the Oceanic Building in 1961. (*David Winyard collection*)

Noise levels seemed to rise higher than the aircraft themselves with the arrival of the Comet. (*David Winyard collection*)

London Heathrow Airport fully operational in 1956. (*Author's collection*)

These buses took passengers from the West London Air Terminal to Heathrow.
(*David Winyard collection*)

owners would not see it again until they arrived at their destination (hopefully, anyway—
it mostly worked quite well).

The same swooping sensation is still apparent as you drive under that sign; the sound
of the tires on the road surface changes, and the engine sounds different. There is a
noticeable descent to the tunnel's first few lengths before it levels out and then begins
to climb back to the surface. One emerges into a different world at the tunnel's other
end, into the central terminal area. Going in the opposite direction has always seemed
something of an anti-climax.

Given the time it had taken to bring the airport to this state—with constant building
work and ever-increasing passenger loads—it was no surprise that the airport was costing
the British taxpayer a lot of money. As early as 1961, a highly critical report on the
London airports was issued by a House of Commons select committee; it recommended
the setting up of a single Airports Authority much like the Port of London Authority,
which managed London's docks, or for that matter, the Port Authority of New York and
New Jersey, which manages the area's airports in addition to its docks.

The Airports Authority Bill was introduced in 1965, receiving Royal Assent on 2 June.
The new organisation was to be named The British Airports Authority—or, more simply,
the BAA. The vesting date (the date on which the BAA would take over ownership and
management of all three London airports and Prestwick, Scotland) was 1 April 1966.

The organisation's first chairman was Peter Masefield, one of Britain's leading aviation figures. Coincidentally, he had ridden a bicycle along the quiet country lanes that ran around the tiny village of Heathrow as a Cambridge University graduate, starting work in the design office at the Fairey Aerodrome in 1935. By his own admission, Masefield had been surprised to be asked to chair an organisation that would have had its work cut out to turn a sclerotic and government-run bureaucracy into an efficient, profit-making enterprise. However, he had enjoyed a successful period serving as the Chief Executive of BEA from 1949 to 1955, and he knew aviation well.

By the mid-'60s, the amount of cargo passing through Heathrow was increasing even more dramatically than passenger numbers, and it had become obvious that the central area would not be big enough to handle freight as well. A new site was therefore set aside on the southern edge of the airport, with Runway No. 5 (or 09 Right/27 Left, if you prefer) to one side of it and the village of Stanwell on the other. Since much of this cargo was carried on passenger aircraft, a 3,000-foot-long tunnel was dug under Runway No. 5 from the central area to the new cargo buildings.

As people arrived at, departed from, or swooped into the central area, they couldn't fail to notice the continual building work. As recommended by the Millbourn Committee, construction had begun on the third passenger terminal during the same year that BAA took ownership.

As one arrived at the airport, the terminal intended for BEA appeared on the left. The new building was built at a cost of £11 million, and it was the largest airport terminal in Europe at the time. It entered use in 1968, initially undertaking domestic services and flights to the Channel Islands and Republic of Ireland. The terminal was fully operational by April 1969, handling all of BEA's flights in addition to those of the Irish airline Aer Lingus. The terminal was officially opened once again by Queen Elizabeth, who named the building 'Terminal 1'. This spelled the end for the evocative names of the other two terminals; the Europa Building, which Her Majesty had opened just fourteen years earlier, became 'Terminal 2', while the Oceanic Building became 'Terminal 3'. For the most part, the three terminals were simply called 'T1', 'T2', and 'T3'. Imagination has never been the strong point of planners and bureaucrats, but it would have been more descriptive for the names to have remained.

T1, T2, and T3—these designations do have the advantage of simplicity, and they might be easier to understand for those who have never travelled by air before. However, for some observers, a little of the post-war aviation glamour began to slip away from the airport. Despite this, and although the central area was beginning to look a little cramped, Heathrow was working well. Alongside the three modern and fully functioning terminals (all neatly within the central area), new multi-story car parks were opened.

The airport still had four runways, although for the most part only the east–west runways (Nos 1 and 5) were used. BEA and BOAC's huge maintenance bases were on the eastern side of the airport, at Hatton Cross, and it was relatively easy for passengers to find which terminal they needed. Services to Europe, domestic services by BEA, and Aer Lingus services used T1; all European airlines used T2; and all long-distance airlines (including BOAC) flew from T3.

As well as the roof gardens, even the Oceanic Building's piers had spectator access.
(*David Winyard collection*)

The Oceanic Building. (*David Winyard*)

BEA NEWS

Number 102
Friday, November 1, 1968

THE FINAL EIGHT:
SEE PAGE FOUR

THE GIANT OPENS ITS DOORS

HEATHROW Airport's Terminal 1 — one of the biggest, best and most badly needed passenger buildings in Europe — is due to open its automatic doors to the public for the first time on Wednesday.

There will be no fanfares, because only half the building is being opened. The red carpet is to stay rolled up until the official opening of the entire terminal, next Spring.

But to give the airlines some benefit from the new building as soon as possible one half has been completely finished, and from Wednesday onwards all BEA InterBritain services will depart from Terminal 1.

However, not all of them will arrive there. One of the quaint anomalies of this "half a terminal is better than none" situation is that because Customs clearance facilities are to be built into the "other half," passengers from the Republic of Ireland and the Channel Islands will temporarily arrive at Terminal 2.

CERTIFICATES

First flight to depart from the new building will be BE 5362 to Edinburgh at 0740—a Vanguard flight. Passengers on this and all other services which use the terminal on Wednesday will be given certificates by the British Airports Authority.

The terminal is to be used by the British short and medium-haul airlines, which means, of course, that all BEA flights will operate to and from Terminal 1 when it is opened for international services as well.

A first glimpse of the new building will be seen by viewers of the Michael Aspel show on BBC television, Monday. Six BEA passenger service girls are likely to be assigned to help during filming for this programme.

For some time members of BEA staff who will work in the building have gone in small groups to be shown round. They have a vital, none-too-easy task ahead of them, because passengers unaccustomed to the new surroundings will expect the staff to know their way round blindfold.

In addition, staff members will need to become used to the several types of new equipment BEA has provided in the building. Equipment designed to make things easier for the staff and better for passengers.

SIZE

Notable among this new equipment is FIND—Flight Information Display—which has been designed and developed by BEA specialists. There is a new intercom system, one of the most extensive in Europe and, in a few months' time, the widespread introduction of PALC, featuring a computerised check-in system which is so clever that, like FIND, it makes the layman's mind boggle.

Almost certainly the first thing that will strike people visiting the terminal for the first time will be the size of the departure area on the first floor and of arrivals on ground level. Compared with Terminal 2 the new building is a giant.

Many of its facilities are aggressive; some are among the best in the world.

Inside Terminal 1—report and pictures in next week's BEA News.

Airline links with Transfreight '69

BEA is involved in two ways in an important exhibition, entitled "Transfreight '69," which was opened in Belfast on Tuesday and was due to end today.

One of the links is that BEA's Manager Northern Ireland, Mr. John Bevan, has organised the venture in his capacity as Chairman of the development and transport committee of the Northern Ireland Chamber of Commerce and Industry.

The second is that on Tuesday Mr. David Coltman, Superintendent of the BEA International Cargo Advisory Bureau, addressed a meeting at the exhibition and that today BEA's Mr. H. N. Murray was representing air cargo during an open discussion of the various freight transport services by air, rail, road and sea.

The new Terminal 1 at night.
Picture: Alistair Philip.

Advertising gives boost to BEA's growing hotel service

BEA is stepping up its fast-growing Hotel Reservation Service, which enables passengers to book flights and hotel accommodation at the same time, and at no extra cost.

BEA has made hotel reservations for its passengers for some time, but this little-known service has been expanding in leaps and bounds during the year as more hotels have been included. Several classes of hotel are available to passengers, who can use the service directly or via their travel agent.

More than 600 selected hotels in Britain and on the Continent are now taking part in this remarkable service, which has been extended to most of the big business centres on the network.

Three hundred of the hotels are in the UK and Ireland—about 50 of them in London—and the remainder are on the Continent. Most have agreed to operate the service on a freesale basis, which means that bookings can be confirmed right away.

Airport Catering Services, the joint BEA/Forte company plays a part in the new service. Its hotels include the Excelsior at Birmingham Airport which opens officially next month, the Excelsior at Manchester, the Phoenicia and Imperial in Malta and the three leading Paris hotels of which controlling interest was recently acquired—the George V, La Trémoille and the Plaza Athénée.

The Hotel Reservation Service is being promoted by BEA both in Britain and internationally as part of the autumn advertising campaign, by direct mail and with full page advertisements in several leading magazines and newspapers. Booklets and brochures telling more about the new system will be out this month.

NEW LIVERY FOR CAMBRIAN

A new livery for Cambrian Airways was shown for the first time this week. Main feature is an up-dated and jet-styled Cambrian dragon.

British Air Services italic lettering appears for the first time on the aircraft fuselage. This same styling will be applied to aircraft of BKS (Cambrian's sister airline in BAS) in due course.

Cambrian Chairman Mr. John Davies also announced this week that the airline planned to operate three new routes next year: London-

Girls on parade in Dublin

Normally BEA has no passenger service girls at Dublin Airport, but on special occasions there are three. Because "town office" girls Helen Burke-Kennedy, Hilary Finlay and Anne O'Brien have uniforms in their wardrobes. And they wore them on Saturday to welcome delegates to the Association of British Travel Agents conference, arriving by Trident. Also there to greet them was Manager Republic of Ireland, Mr. W. Matheson.

A 1968 edition of BEA's newspaper reveals all; BEA gets its own home. (*Author's collection*)

BEA's maintenance area in 1955. (*David Winyard collection*)

Inside the Europa Building. (*Stephan Parfitt collection*)

The Queen's Building airside. Note the popularity of the roof gardens. (Stephan Parfitt collection)

A BEA Vickers Vanguard represented just one of the many aircraft visible from the roof gardens. (*Stephan Parfitt collection*)

The Queen's Building from the tower. Note the Soviet Tupolev jet upper centre and the pre-war DC3 beyond it. Russian *sang-froid* and Western propeller power face each other head-on. (*Stephan Parfitt collection*)

Four BEA Vanguards contrast with the Scandinavian Airlines French-built Caravelle. (*David Winyard collection*)

Land Rovers and baggage trolleys. The tunnel (upper right) was one of several that were intended to be used by ground vehicles to access the more remote areas of the apron, reducing the risk of collisions between aircraft and vehicles. They proved to be unnecessary. (*David Winyard collection*)

The roof gardens remained a well-used attraction into the 1980s. (*Stephan Parfitt collection*)

The Oceanic Building. (*Stephan Parfitt collection*)

The Oceanic Building's frontage allowed more natural light to enter the terminal than its earlier counterpart. (*Stephan Parfitt collection*)

The new terminal granted much needed relief to BOAC and the other airlines once it opened. The Iranian Boeing 727 in the background had a long trip from Tehran. (*David Winyard*)

Over the course of just twenty-three years, from 1946 to 1969, London Heathrow had become the busiest international airport in the world. Some airports had more aircraft movements (particularly those in the USA), and some even had higher passenger numbers, but none had more traffic to and from other countries.

Nevertheless, aviation was a constantly evolving business. New ways of doing things often arrived with mind-boggling speed, sometimes immediately after the last 'new' development. The only constant factors were the ever-increasing loudness of the aircraft, their growing numbers at Heathrow, and their dramatic increases in size.

4
Boeing's Beast

The Boeing 747 is the commuter train of the global village.

Hendrik Tennekes, *The Simple Science of Flight*, 1996

The explosive growth in air travel during the early 1960s caught even the eternally optimistic and always forward-looking commercial aviation industry somewhat by surprise. Airlines had ordered new jet aircraft (like the Boeing 707 and the Douglas DC8) in large numbers from the end of the 1950s into the '60s, and in the heady days of the new decade, airlines actually owned the aircraft they operated and were still paying for them. Over the twenty years since 1945, the rapid development of aviation meant that airlines were obliged to frequently buy new types of aircraft in order to stay competitive—even in a tightly regulated marketplace. This cost them a huge amount of money, but they also enjoyed huge revenues. Even so, it always took a long time to pay off the debt—even with the continual increase in passenger numbers, particularly on flights to and from Heathrow.

It wasn't only long-haul routes that were booming. The London to Paris route is the oldest scheduled route in existence, and it saw significant growth in this period. Air France had acquired new, French-built twin-engine Caravelle jetliners, and BEA had bought the British-built Hawker Siddeley Trident, which used three engines clustered around the tail.

There were still plenty of propellers to be seen (and heard), but to the enthusiastic observer this was the period that represented Heathrow at its greatest—at least in terms of variety of aircraft type.

I made my first long-haul flight from Heathrow, flying with BOAC from London to New York aboard one of the first (although regrettably not *the* first) BOAC Super VC10 services. This was a time when airlines publicised their new aircraft as much as their on-board service, and sometimes even more so. BOAC pronounced: 'The most comfortable economy seat in the world is on the VC 10'. Later, even more grandly, they stated:

There's more to this jetliner than meets the eye—it's easy on the ears. There are many ways to describe the quietness in the BOAC VC10. When you fly in the BOAC VC10, it really is quiet … the four powerful Rolls-Royce jet engines are at the tail end so all the jet noise gets carried away behind you.

As those outside, behind, and below the aircraft could confirm, he British-built airliner was ear-splittingly loud. Nevertheless, by any yardstick, the Vickers VC10 was a good-looking aircraft. It was built at Brooklands (near Weybridge, Surrey), which is not far from Heathrow and was once a racetrack for the best of British racing cars. Decades later, the mere thought of this elegant airliner continues to make some people go misty-eyed.

Despite its aesthetically pleasing design, the VC10 had a fuel-consumption problem; heavier than competing designs, its weight meant that it used a lot of fuel. Its four Rolls-Royce engines at the rear, along with its tall, sweeping fin with the tail wings perched at the top, also meant that the aircraft was tail-heavy, but they did result in a quiet ride once you were inside one. The principal design purpose of the VC10 was to connect London to Britain's far-flung yet steadily shrinking empire, where some airports (such as those in Africa) did not have long runways. With the engines situated at the back, there was nothing to get in the way of the flaps and slats on the wings, giving them extra lift at low speeds. However, the UK was handing independence to many of these countries during this period, and this meant the number of flights BOAC were carrying out would drop. The VC10's unique characteristics no longer suited the needs of BOAC, which turned its attention to the Boeing 707. The US-built aircraft was cheaper to operate and had a better range compared to the VC10, which was not ideal for long over-water crossings.

Vickers then tailored the design more closely to BOAC's needs and came up with the Super VC10, a slightly longer version of the original with a bigger capacity for passengers. It proved more suitable for BOAC's services to North America and elsewhere, but less so for other airlines. The design alterations also resulted in the both versions of the VC10, Standard and Super, entering service later than the 707 and DC8, and the world's airlines were already committing to either Boeing or Douglas. As a state-owned airline, however, BOAC were obliged to buy the VC10 in the same way that BEA were obliged to buy the Trident; both aircraft suffered from the fact that they were built to fit the needs of the two UK national airlines, thus significantly reducing the potential for sales to other airlines around the world. BEA even wanted to order the Boeing 727 for its European network, but the British government ordered the company to buy the Trident instead.

Aside from its weight and fuel-consumption issues, the VC10 was operationally considered to be a better aircraft than the Boeing 707, but as a result of the design changes, the aircraft was not a success commercially around the world in terms of sales—just like the Trident. Despite the disappointment for both Vickers and Hawker Siddeley, the state-owned airlines continued to operate their British-built aircraft from Heathrow for over twenty years.

In addition to the sales issues, both aircraft were extremely noisy. Luckily for the passengers, the VC10 and Trident shared the design of rear-fuselage-mounted engines, meaning the jets' decibels were less noticeable in the cabin. However, the residents around Heathrow and in West London could always tell when a BOAC or BEA flight was taking off or coming in.

Meanwhile, Boeing and Douglas had designed their aircraft to appeal to as many of its potential customers (the airlines) as possible, and it showed. BOAC reached a compromise with the British government, and as well as both versions of the VC10, they also acquired a fleet of Boeing 707s powered by Rolls-Royce engines, which were at least built in Britain, even if the aircraft itself was manufactured in the USA by Boeing. Almost all the other airlines bought 707s and DC8s with US-made Pratt and Whitney engines.

The economics of jets made difference to the way in which the airlines operated. The increased fuel economy and greater load-carrying capacity (both passengers and cargo) meant lower fares; this meant more people could afford to buy tickets. How else could my father and I afford to go to America, or Paris? We went to the French capital twice and visited Munich once, travelling on BEA Tridents outward on both occasions. Returning from Munich (travelling to Paris for the second time), we rode in a Caravelle operated by JAT Yugoslav Airlines, on the second leg of a service from Belgrade to Paris Orly Airport.

These trips took place during a time when gentlemen wore ties (even my father) and ladies wore dresses and carried a handbag demurely in their arm. Fares had come steeply down compared to the 1950s, when air travel was usually the preserve of the well-to-do, but despite the increasing numbers, there was still a certain decorum amongst those who travelled by air. Looking around the Europa Building (and definitely the Oceanic Building) at Heathrow, one would see a lot of ties and handbags. When the Beatles caused chaos by departing or arriving through Heathrow, even they wore ties; the only denim on display was worn by the screaming masses who packed the Queen's Building roof gardens to see them.

The Douglas Aircraft Company (based in Long Beach, California) realised that they could do quite a lot with the DC8 as the design matured. As Vickers had discovered with the VC10, Douglas found that they could make the fuselage longer—even more so than the VC10, in fact. This meant more seats, more passengers, and more revenue. Douglas's ultimate version of the DC8 was the DC8-60 series, also known as the 'Stretch Eight'. The Boeing 707 was less easily extended due to the way it was designed, and Douglas outsold their competitors for a time. However, Boeing had something else in mind as far as size was concerned.

Boeing ultimately sold more 707s than Douglas sold DC8s, but the DC8 lasted much longer in airline service. Some examples received new, quieter, less fuel-thirsty engines and remained in service until the late 1980s, by which time the 707 had been retired by most of the airlines that operated the type.

By 1966 people were flying in greater numbers than ever before, and there were only two ways left for airlines to increase capacity. The first was to buy more aircraft and schedule more flights; the problem with this was that airports were reaching their limits as far as handling aircraft numbers were concerned. The only other way was to make the actual aircraft bigger.

On 14 April 1966, Juan Trippe, Pan American's legendary chairman, signed an order for an airliner that was twice as big as the stretch DC8. The aircraft had only come into being as an airliner because Boeing had lost out on a US Air Force contract to Lockheed's giant Galaxy military transporter. In converting their prototype to civil use, Boeing changed the face of the airline industry in one fell swoop. The change had immediate consequences for the world's airports—including London Heathrow.

The Boeing 747 was huge, and it still is now. Take a Battle of Britain Spitfire fighter. If you stand next to it, it's bigger than you are, but at least it's clearly human-sized. Now stand under the nose of a Douglas DC3, which revolutionised air travel back in the pre-Second World War days. Its nose will seem to tower over you, but at the back, where one enters the aircraft, it is far less dominating. Each passing generation of aircraft had been succeeded by an increase in size and power, and yet the 747's scale was utterly overwhelming.

Watching one take off can be mind-boggling—especially at close quarters. How does something this big get off the ground? How does it stay in the air? How can those tiny

Almost home. A BEA Trident on short finals.
(*Richard Briggs*)

The dawn of a new decade. The Boeing 707's position as the aircraft of choice for long-haul services is about to be usurped by the 747. A pair of Pan Am 707-321s, a single TWA example on its take-off roll and a BOAC 707-436, seem blissfully unaware of the looming giant. (*Richard Briggs*)

Medium haul at Terminal 2; Olympic from Greece (left) and Air France make an odd fit with the ungainly Air France Bruguet Deux Ponts cargo hauler (centre) ambling past. (*Richard Briggs*)

Above: Heathrow's wide open spaces in the early 1970s. A Swissair DC9 sits next to one of the airline's four-engine Convair jetliners, with a KLM DC8 at the end as a BOAC VC10 climbs out. (*Richard Briggs*)

Below: Olympic Airways arrives from Athens. The hangars in the background will be replaced by Terminal 4 within ten years. (*Author*)

Terminal 1's international pier gets longer as
British Airways fins steadily replace BEA ones.
(*Richard Briggs*)

Some of BA's Tridents were never fully repainted into BA colours before retirement. Old and new
colours at T1. (*Richard Briggs*)

Two in one; a BA fin and a BOAC window line on one of the carrier's Boeing 747-136 aircraft. (*Richard Briggs*)

figures in the bulge at the front, on top of the fat fuselage, control this thing, and how can they possibly land it? Despite the questions asked at the time, the aircraft did take off, stay in the air, and stay under control. It even managed to land safely.

Pan Am put the 747 into service from New York to Heathrow on 12 January 1970. Both JFK and Heathrow had extended their terminals to handle this behemoth, and other airports around the world were doing the same. In order to allow the 747 to fit at T3, Runway No. 6 (15/33), directly in front of the terminal, was finally taken out of use, as the Millbourn Committee had earlier suggested. The runway in front of T1 had already been paved over to provide space for the piers of the building, which was still less than two years old. T1's piers now stretched across the path of the former runway, leaving Heathrow with four usable runways.

Since it had become very obvious very quickly that LHR was going to simultaneously handle more 747s than most airports, a long pier connecting the terminal with a cross pier (like a letter 'T') was placed where the runway had been, with the gates and aircraft stands located along the cross pier. Terminal 3 itself was also expanded, with a separate arrivals building rising next to the original, which became reserved for departures.

BOAC's introduction to the 747 was delayed when air crew declined to fly the new type unless they received an increase in pay. Even before the construction of T3's extensions had finished, the cross pier (originally intended to handle just seven of the new wide-body jets) was lengthened at its northern end to take ten aircraft. This brought the pier too close to Runway No. 7 for the concrete strip to remain in use; it was closed too, being used for additional remote aircraft parking including 747s and smaller aircraft. Buses were used to take passengers to the terminal. Heathrow now had just three runways—the mainly used east–west pair (Nos 1 and 5) and the remaining crosswind runway (No. 2).

The BAA's portfolio of airports also increased at this time, with Edinburgh being handed over to the authority. They were charged with the task of virtually rebuilding the airport,

Boeing's beast arrives in 1970. This was the first 747 service, operated by Pan Am from New York JFK. (*David Winyard*)

and they began doing this by laying down a new runway and terminal. At the time, there was no opposition to a new runway—if there was, it did not make national news.

From 1971–72 there were 13,000 movements at Heathrow by what had become known as 'wide-bodied' airliners, with the 747 about to be joined by the Douglas DC10 and the Lockheed L1011 TriStar. Both the latter types were smaller than the 747 but still considerably larger than the 707 and DC8.

In 1973, the oil-producing countries in the Middle East increased the price of oil by 70 per cent, sending shockwaves reverberating around the world and causing a crisis in commercial aviation. Suddenly, fuel wasn't cheap any more. Ticket prices went up, load factors (the number of passengers and the amount of cargo carried) dropped alarmingly, and airlines that had gone deep into debt to buy wide-bodied aircraft found themselves in equally deep financial trouble. All big corporations carry debt, but even though expenditure may well exceed income for a time, such are the size of airline revenues, even in a downturn, that most carriers were able to continue in business despite huge losses. Some were yet to fully pay for the fleets of 707s and DC8s they had bought during the previous decade. Even so, since many airlines were state-owned (like BOAC and BEA), their governments continued to fund the financial shortfalls. From 1974–75, for the first time since the airport had opened, passenger figures at LHR actually fell.

The early 1970s were not turning out to be kind to the aviation industry. Hijacks, spiralling costs, and a drop in the numbers of people flying caused big losses for airlines and airports. Nevertheless, the future is always rosy for an airline executive—particularly if they have an understanding bank manager. If a large corporation goes out of business, their mammoth debt becomes unrecoverable if the assets that remain are worth less than the amount owed. In the case of the air transport industry, the result of an airline going bankrupt, especially a large one, usually results in a glut of second-hand aircraft flooding an already saturated market. The result is that assets once highly prized—big new aircraft, in this instance—lose their value rapidly.

Nevertheless, the airline world is a robust one, with upturns always following downturns. Even in the early 1970s, the industry had a level of financial optimism that mere mortals can only dream of. This optimism encouraged a number of European countries (including the UK) to join forces and create a new company with a new product aimed at the short-haul and medium-haul market (the long-haul routes were being operated by the 747). The appropriately named 'European Airbus' consortium designed and built a wide-bodied airliner for these routes, a market previously dominated by smaller aircraft like the Boeing 727 and 737, Britain's BAC111 (which sold well around the world), and the Douglas DC9.

The Douglas DC10 and the Lockheed TriStar also had shorter-range capability, but their primary target was the huge US domestic market, particularly on coast-to-coast services and similar routes. This didn't stop both aircraft selling worldwide (especially the DC10). BEA came under pressure to buy the new Airbus aircraft as a substantial number of its parts were to be built in Britain. However, they had already committed to acquiring the TriStar, with Heathrow–Paris as one of its primary route markets. The BEA order for the Lockheed aircraft had been allowed by the British government because its engines were again manufactured in the UK by Rolls-Royce (RR).

The optimism in Europe was bolstered by Air France's state-ownership and the payment of its bills by the taxpayer; thus it was the French national carrier who put the first Airbus A300 into service, using the type on the Paris–London route on 23 May 1974. Meanwhile, LHR continued to extend and rebuild. As Peter Masefield succinctly put it, it was 'alterations as usual during business'.

The arrival of the Airbus meant the now twenty-year-old Terminal 2 needed improvements. The most visible of these changes involved the placing of two exterior pedestrian walkways on the front, like a pair of bright-white, slightly robotic worms hanging onto the building. They took passengers and their baggage trolleys out of the terminal building when they needed to move between floors, thus freeing up space inside to handle the A300's bigger passenger numbers.

The Vickers Viscount first whistled its way into LHR in the 1950s, its turbo-prop engines sounding very distinctive. This excellent little aircraft had managed to remain in service with BEA and into the new era of British Airways; in 1974, one took my father and me to Jersey. Heathrow had by this time gained something of an unfortunate reputation for industrial action by its unions. The term 'industrial action' has always seemed something of a misnomer; if you're on strike, you aren't being overly active. This was particularly true of baggage handlers, who seemed especially prone to withdrawing their labour and often at short notice or even no notice at all. As we checked in for our flight to the Channel Islands (having arrived on a Lufthansa Boeing 737-130 from Cologne at T2), the handlers had gone on strike by the time we arrived at the gate. We all sat in the departure lounge for a while until the Viscount's captain appeared to tell everybody that the aircraft was ready to go—minus bags. 'However,' he said, 'if anyone would care to load them, we can go.' Being airside, loading your own bags into the hold of an airliner, is either a tedious imposition (if you're an eager holidaymaker, raring to go) or a mere bagatelle. If you are an airport-crazed child, however, it's heaven.

The Viscount's bigger stablemate, the Vanguard, came onto the scene too late to sell in any great numbers. Jets like the BAC111 and Boeing 737, along with Douglas's DC9, were now *de rigueur* on short-haul flights. Apart from BEA, Air Canada was the only

1976. The grainy early efforts of a boyish enthusiast to capture T1's international pier from the roof gardens. British Airways had been formed by this point, but most of the aircraft still carried BEA's markings—except for the BAC111 and Trident hiding in the middle. Note the young aviation fan at the bottom left. (*Author*)

One of Air France's new Airbus A300 wide bodies. With the arrival of bigger aircraft at T2, three stands replaced the four previously available and the pier itself was been modified to handle the greater number of passengers using it. In the background, a BA 747 soars into the air. (*Author*)

Terminal 2's piers. Note the enlarged gate rooms on the nearest of the two piers. (*Author*)

Terminal 2 again. A soon-to-be-retired BA 707 lifts off behind a row of Europeans. (*Author*)

airline to buy the Vanguard. Affectionately nicknamed 'The Mudguard', it served BEA well throughout the 1960s before entering a second life with the airline as a freighter. By the time of our return from Jersey, just one Vanguard was left in passenger service; after it had brought us back to Heathrow, it began hauling cargo as well.

On a purely personal level, I felt I now had a stake in Heathrow. I had flown on one of the first BOAC Super VC10 services, I had loaded bags, and I had been one of those on board the last passenger-carrying Vanguard, yet I was still nowhere near adulthood. All I needed now was to fly on Boeing's big beast—the 747.

Heathrow's traffic had recovered by 1977, and the airport overtook the Port of London to become the busiest port in Britain in terms of value of goods carried. Twenty-four million people passed through the airport. In December, the Piccadilly Line of the London Underground opened its extension to Hatton Cross, later extending under and into the central area. With road access to the airport becoming more congested and time-consuming, the line gave travellers an alternative option. Heathrow's continued success, expansion, and inclusion in the underground network proved that the optimism inherent within the airline industry was well-founded.

By 1978, Heathrow was full. It has been full ever since, and it's been full for so long that the idea of it not being full seems fanciful. The three terminals and aircraft parking areas were constantly running at capacity. With the barriers to expanding transatlantic travel disappearing rapidly, airlines like Delta and American Airlines, Air New Zealand, Cathay Pacific, and Freddie Laker's Skytrain and its US equivalent, People Express, had to use Gatwick—whether they wanted to or not. The demand for air travel services to London was rising, and fares were coming down again. The days when people wore ties when flying had not quite vanished, but they were going and going rapidly.

Gatwick, already serving most of the charter and holiday traffic to and from the south east of England, as well as the newly arrived legacy carriers, was now at the forefront of long-haul, low-fare travel. Fares continued to drop and the number of flights increased so quickly that for some, it was like getting on a bus. Businessmen still wore ties; first class was still first class, and economy was economy.

The Heathrow–Gatwick Airlink service was brought into use in the same year. For those who landed at either Heathrow or Gatwick and needed to get to the other airport (and who had the money), the helicopter was the only way to go. Apart from anything else, it was different and exciting—for businessmen and for me. The helicopter flights were run by British Caledonian, who were based at Gatwick and carving a name for themselves as the UK's 'second-force' airline. They served routes that British Airways would not serve from Heathrow (for one reason or another). To fill spare seats on the Airlink, British Caledonian (or BCAL, as they were often known) would offer cheap return tickets for anyone who wanted to go on a helicopter. I was one of many who took a trip from Gatwick to Heathrow and back. It is the only time I have flown on a helicopter, although some have suggested that helicopters don't fly at all—they are so ugly that the earth simply repels them.

When the M25 orbital motorway around London opened, connecting the two airports, anti-noise protestors called for the end of the Airlink service; its flights ended in February 1986.

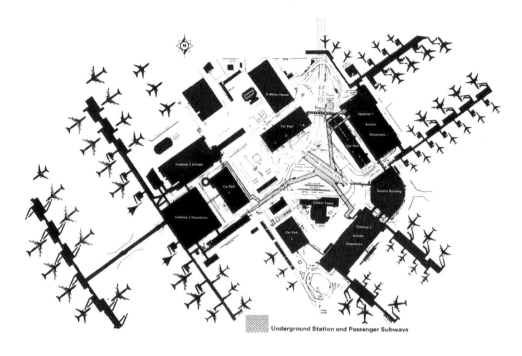

From a 1983 publicity brochure plan of the central area. (BAA/*Author's collection*)

The subterranean passages linking the London Underground with all three terminals in 1983. (BAA/*Author's collection*)

5

The Rocket

You can be in London at 10 o'clock and in New York at 10 o'clock. I have never found another way of being in two places at once.

Sir David Frost

I never flew on Concorde. It was never called 'The Concorde'—just 'Concorde'. The sleek supersonic airliner was so unique that no prefix was ever needed. Designed and built jointly by the British Aircraft Corporation (BAC) in Britain and Aerospatiale in France, it was the world's only successful supersonic airliner. It entered service with a flight between London Heathrow and Bahrain on 21 January 1976—thirty years after the first departure from Heathrow.

British Airways' first destination was Bahrain because that was where the money was in 1976. At the exact same time as British Airways began their Concorde service with G-BOAA at Heathrow, Air France began their Concorde service with F-BVFA flying from Paris Charles de Gaulle (CDG) to Dakar, West Africa, and then on to Rio de Janeiro, Brazil.

The stop at Dakar was necessary pick up extra fuel. Concorde was never truly capable of long-range flights; it was primarily meant to be used between London, Paris, and New York, along with the few other routes that could really warrant such an expensive, premium service, like Brussels–New York, Frankfurt–New York, and Tehran–London. Why Tehran? At the time, Iran was a rich ally of the West. The Shah of Iran, who would soon be overthrown and replaced by the Ayatollah Khomeini, declared that he would buy two aircraft, with London being the preferred destination for them.

The aircraft was extraordinarily expensive to develop, expensive to build, expensive to purchase, and expensive to operate. The amount of taxpayer's money spent on it was truly mind-boggling. The only way that BOAC (and then British Airways) were able to acquire their fleet was for the British government to write off the costs, essentially gifting the fleet to the airline.

During its gestation period, Concorde was not the only supersonic airliner under development; however, it did turn out to be the only workable design. The Soviet Union's Tupolev TU-144 was never as operationally sound as Concorde—it was effectively a poor copy, and it suffered a career-ending crash in front of a worldwide audience at the June 1973 Paris Air Show. The TU-144 enjoyed a brief spell as a freighter between

Moscow and Alma Aty before vanishing from sight. Meanwhile, the US could only build a wooden mock-up before the money ran out.

Since Concorde was conceived in an era when fuel was cheap and prestige had no limit, its high price was not really a surprise. What raised eyebrows more was that the British and French governments actually agreed to do it. At one point, the British wanted to drop the whole thing due to the increasing financial drain. However, the cost of compensating the French was even more frightening, so they stuck with it for the duration. The agreement they had signed with France gave a manufacture date of November 1962, and it was an *entente cordiale* that only just endured. In fact, it would be December 1967 before the first prototype was rolled out in France, and it took nine more years to get it into service.

All aircraft, both civil and military, undergo a prolonged and comprehensive testing phase before entering service. This testing is especially necessary for civilian airliners; if a design flaw in a new aircraft causes it to crash and kill people, it is not good for sales. By a distance, Concorde was tested more than any new aircraft before or since.

BAC and Aerospatiale were breaking new ground with Concorde. After testing it beyond the pale, they then had to sell it. BOAC and Air France were naturally obliged to acquire the new aircraft, but other sales were a little thin on the ground.

All the major airlines declared their interest in it—Sabena of Belgium, Germany's Lufthansa, and QANTAS (especially given the distance between Australia and everywhere else). Even the mighty Pan American and TWA in the USA wanted to acquire Concorde—the fact that their own country's SST was so far behind meant that they would be uncompetitive if they didn't acquire the aircraft. A large number of airlines took out options to buy, and potential sales looked good.

Options are one of the peculiarities of ordering an airliner. They don't actually commit an airline to really buying or placing an order to buy; they merely give an indication of the airline's interest in buying. On the other hand, it gives an airline an early place in the queue to receive an aircraft when orders are actually placed. Signing up to early options can allow airlines to receive their aircraft ahead of their competitors. However, none of the airlines who had taken options on Concorde ended up purchasing the aircraft; in the end, it would cost them too much. It wasn't so much the purchase price, although that was high enough to begin with. As the test aircraft were put through their paces, the operating costs began to mount.

Not only was Concorde spectacularly expensive, it was also spectacularly loud— at least to some. Despite the fact it represented the ultimate in commercial airliner technology, it was a little disconcerting for the public living beneath flight paths to be told that Concorde would demonstrate its speed by shattering windows and eardrums as it flew past (most such stories, although having some truth to them, were greatly exaggerated by news media). It wasn't just that the engines were loud, either. When any supersonic aircraft approaches and breaks the speed of sound, the resulting shockwaves cause a loud sonic boom that is easily heard and felt on the ground. Governments around the world began banning the aircraft from going supersonic over their territory. The increasing number of restrictions, combined with the high price point, meant that the airlines began to cancel their options one by one, never placing actual orders to buy.

In New York, where the residents were perhaps a little peeved that Concorde was not American, protesters made more noise than the aircraft did. They managed to temporarily attain a ban on Concorde flights into JFK, but it was subsequently overturned. The demonstrations were always at their loudest when the protesters knew Concorde was coming over on one of its numerous test flights. One day, BA flew one into New York without telling anyone they were going to. Nobody noticed. It is an undeniable fact that Concorde made more noise than any other aircraft; however, when one is amongst many aircraft (as at JFK or Heathrow), for the most part nobody realises when one aircraft is louder than another. In this particular instance, Concorde landed at JFK, sat on the ground for a while, and then departed—with not a protester in sight.

The aircraft had other difficulties to contend with, and two in particular. The first was the stratospheric rise in the price of oil during the early 1970s. The second difficulty was the fact that by the time BA and Air France made their simultaneous departures in 1976, the Boeing 747 had established itself as the workhorse of long-haul air routes—along with the later versions of the Douglas DC10 and Lockheed L1011 TriStar.

What made the 747 so different was the number of people that could be herded into it. Its economics were so awesomely more advantageous that using a Concorde on a similar route made no sense at all. The only people who benefitted were those who wanted to get from London to New York in three hours, not the seven hours and thirty minutes it took on a 747—and those who had the money to pay the fare.

In order to convince enough people to accept the high cost of flying on Concorde, Air France arranged an event to demonstrate the aircraft's spectacular speed. One of the French carrier's aircraft took off from Boston to Paris at the same time as one of the company's 747s departed Paris, travelling in the opposite direction. Concorde reached Paris while the 747 was still over the Atlantic. It landed, spent one hour and eight minutes on the ground, and then departed again, heading back to Boston. The plane landed there eleven minutes ahead of the still-inbound 747. It was the ultimate civilian rocket.

However, once Concorde was cleared to fly into JFK, other destinations didn't last long. At Miami, this led to a close encounter between the rocket and a Pan American Boeing 727 with myself on board. It was 1986, and I was on a trip to the US. Halfway between Miami and my flight to Washington, D.C., the captain told the passengers that Concorde would be passing not too high above us. I had my window seat and my camera, but no film; I'd used it up on my departure from Miami. The most important lesson for an aspiring photographer is to always carry a camera and spare film (or memory cards today) for an unexpected moment. Still, BA's arrow looked undeniably beautiful as it sped by.

Washington was the other long-surviving route from both Heathrow and Paris until it too was dropped. This left Heathrow and Paris to JFK as the only route on which the ordinary person could fly faster than a speeding bullet—providing they had the money.

The sleek airliner never wore the dark-blue colours and gold Speedbird of BOAC. By 1976, the merger between BOAC and BEA had created British Airways, and the new airline became Britain's flag-carrier. The delta-winged flagship therefore had the red quarter-flag design on its tail, although the merged airline did retain a small, dark-blue Speedbird by the nose on all aircraft.

One BA Concorde had Singapore Airlines colours on its left side while retaining its usual paint on the other. This was for a joint BA/SIA service that extended the Bahrain flights, with plans to later extend the flights to Australia. The trouble was that Concorde was limited to only going supersonic over the sea, which meant that the amount of time saved was not enough to make the flights viable. This rather defeated the purpose of using the aircraft altogether, and the resultant lack of demand ended up causing big losses on the route for both airlines and the enterprise was dropped. Although South African Airways had SAA stickers temporarily applied to a BA Concorde for proposed flights between Heathrow and Johannesburg, Singapore Airlines remain the only airline other than BA and Air France to have a Concorde in its full colour scheme (even if it was only one side).

Braniff Airways also ran a joint service with BA and Air France, extending both carriers' Washington flights to Braniff's Dallas/Fort Worth base. The flights over the US also had to remain subsonic, again making the exercise somewhat pointless (and expensive). The aircraft of both European airlines remained in their usual colour schemes, although temporary US registrations had to be issued and applied to the aircraft for them to be used on domestic US flights. The move gave Braniff a one-aircraft, one-stop, supersonic service from Dallas to London and Paris, but again the take-up wasn't enough to keep the flights running. Braniff went out of business in May 1982.

British Airways Concorde services were profitable for the airline. By using the aircraft on charter flights and a variety of 'specials', the extra revenue generated meant that BA's Concorde operations did make money on the whole. According to the company, the aircraft broke even on flights holding around 40–45 per cent of passenger capacity; in 1985, the average numbers of passengers carried on a flight was as high as 65 per cent (the typical seating capacity was 100). BA used Concorde to win business customers, guaranteeing a certain number of Concorde upgrades in return for corporate accounts with the airline. This was a key factor in taking business away from the company's transatlantic competitors—primarily Pan Am and TWA. Although the carrier never disclosed specific numbers, media reports estimated that the Heathrow–New York service made an annual operating profit of £20 million by the end of the 1990s.

Air France didn't do quite so well. They were never as adept as BA at marketing the glamour of the Rocket, but they did pull off one colourful coup. For a very short time, one of the French carrier's fleet was painted in a special Pepsi-Cola scheme for an advertising feature. The Pepsi-Cola scheme was not used on scheduled services, only for the feature, but they did use their aircraft for charter flights. One of these flights would spell the end for Concorde.

On 25 July 2000, Concorde F-BTSC crashed. It was the only one to ever come down. Flight AF4590 departed Paris Charles De Gaulle *en route* to JFK, carrying a full load of passengers who were due to link up with a cruise ship in New York. As the aircraft sped along the runway, approaching its take-off speed, it struck a piece of metal that is believed to have dropped off a Continental Airlines Douglas DC10 that preceded it. The tyres on the left main gear blew and the debris was thrown up into the wing, puncturing the fuel tanks and causing a fire. By this stage, the aircraft was committed to getting into the air; with its left wing blazing, it crashed onto a hotel southwest of the airport and disintegrated. All 109 people on board were killed, as were four on the ground.

There had been previous incidents involving Concorde, with two being particularly notorious. On 21 March 1992, one of BA's fleet had part of its rudder detach somewhere between London and New York, unbeknownst to the crew; on landing at JFK, they were told by the control tower that a big piece of their aircraft was missing. On 14 June 1979, another Air France Concorde had a tyre blow out on take-off from Washington. As in the later incident, this sent shards of rubber flying through the wing; on this occasion, however, the aircraft avoided the conflagration that would consume the Paris departure. The hole on the wing was noticed by a passenger, who immediately informed the flight crew. The aircraft returned to Washington safely.

Neither of the aircraft had crashed, but the incident at Washington demonstrated Concorde's form for blowing tyres despite all its undeniable beauty. It's not uncommon for aircraft tyres to burst on take-off, and I have seen it happen. On one sunny summer afternoon at Heathrow, I watched as a Lockheed TriStar began its roll along 27 left and burst several tyres. The series of detonations was noticeable even from the rooftop viewing area of the Queen's Building. The TriStar was nowhere near the speed at which it would have to take off, so it slowed and stopped at the far end of the runway. Several fire engines rapidly emerged from their station to go after it. Other than causing all flights to use the other runway—thus resulting in delays—nothing else happened. It was a moment of brief drama, an anti-climax—but no crash.

On 25 July 2000, however, the fire spreading rapidly through the left wing of the Air France flight rendered it unflyable, and it came down. The rest of the Concorde fleets came down with it—both Air France's and BA's.

Any airliner accident is a shock, and particularly one that results in the destruction of the aircraft and the loss of all on board. In this case, part of the shock was due to the fact that there were so few of the type in use. If it had sold in large numbers around the world, the law of averages suggest that somebody would have lost a Concorde before the Air France flight. Despite being one of the safest airlines in the world, Lufthansa was the first to lose a 747—and relatively early in the type's career. One of their fleet crashed after departing Nairobi, Kenya, on 20 November 1974. The aircraft had been in service for less than four years. The crash may have been the first for a 747, but it didn't stop airlines buying more of the type (including Lufthansa), and it didn't stop people flying on them either.

Just like the Comet had done twenty years beforehand, the DC10 experienced several crashes early in its life. One of the worst of these was a Turkish Airlines flight departing Istanbul on 3 March 1974, heading to Paris and then on to Heathrow. After leaving Paris on the final leg of its journey, the rear cargo door burst open, severing the control lines to the tail. The trijet plummeted into Ermenonville Forest, killing 345 people. The rear cargo door had been a problem on the DC10 in the same way that the tyres would be a problem on Concorde. The same issue had occurred on an American Airlines flight over Windsor Locks, USA, but the aircraft had managed to land safely. In May 1979, five years after the Turkish Airlines disaster, an American Airlines DC10 crashed immediately after taking off from Chicago's O'Hare Airport. There had been a number of non-fatal incidents in between the two major ones, but after the crash at O'Hare, the DC10 was grounded worldwide—just as the Comet had been. Nevertheless, the DC10's problems were fixed (as were those of the Comet), and the aircraft went on to serve many airlines around the world for years. This included BA, who inherited eight of them after the 1988 takeover of British Caledonian. I flew on the DC10 with both airlines, and I'm still here.

The difficulty for Concorde was that it was no ordinary aircraft. It was unique, special, and only owned and operated by BA and Air France. It was quick, but it lacked the worldwide use of the 747 and DC10—and all the support that such use brings. This, in addition to Concorde's ruinous cost to operate and travel on, meant that the crash in 2000 affected the type much more than it would have affected the 747 or DC10. It became clear that the problem was due to the wing fuel tanks being too weak to withstand the impact of a shredded tyre, and it was hugely costly for BA and Air France to remedy. Concorde was grounded and had its slender wings clipped until the tanks could be strengthened; however, its return to service was short-lived.

The crash meant rebuilding confidence in the aircraft would take time after it re-entered service, but time ran out when the USA suffered the 9/11 terrorist attacks. Passenger numbers tumbled across all airlines, but Concorde was hit particularly hard.

While BA had made money with Concorde, Air France had not. Aerospatiale had been subsumed into Airbus many years before, and they were the ones now providing spares support for the aircraft. With their own aircraft to look after—the A320, A330, and A340—and the development of the huge A380, it was not worth Airbus's time to spend the cash on the small number of Concorde aircraft in use. As a result, Concorde flights ended in November 2003.

Above: The Rocket—still with a French test registration, but in full BA colours. This photograph was taken during a demonstration visit before the aircraft entered service. (*David Winyard*)

Opposite above: 'To Fly. To Serve.' (*David Winyard*)

Opposite moddle: Terminal 3, before the move to the new T4. (*David Winyard*)

Opposite below: The Rocket's final British Airways colours at T4. (*David Winyard*)

6

Dead Man's Shoes I

I fly because it releases my mind from the tyranny of petty things.

Antoine de Saint-Exupéry

People go to work because they have to, just like they pay taxes because they have to. Most do not like the idea that the government will take some of their money away from them—even if it's a government they elected. In a few cases, the government takes quite a lot, and in most cases it is before you see any of it. However, in order to pay taxes, you must have a job to get taxed on. Many people take a job and hold it (sometimes for life) not because they like it, but because it pays the bills—including their taxes.

Aviation is in the blood; those who work in it often do so because they like being around aircraft. Many of them, myself included, even fill some of their spare time by making plastic model kits of the aircraft they work with (or write about).

Tony Horton is one of these people. In his spare time, he runs the competition at the annual convention of the International Plastic Modellers Society (UK)—or, as it's more usually known, the IPMS (UK). The convention is held every year at Telford, a little way to the north-west of Birmingham and not too far from the English border with Wales.

The IPMS is to be found all over the world, hence its 'International' tag. The show in the UK is by far the world's biggest and best-attended, drawing participants from around the globe. Many of them fly into and out of Heathrow on the way to and from Telford.

To pay his bills, Tony trains baggage handlers at Heathrow. Before his present role, he loaded bags himself; he might even have loaded mine at some point. He's one of those yellow-jacketed people seen diving in and out of the cavernous cargo holds of the BA fleet at Terminal 5. In the US, they are sometimes and somewhat unkindly known as 'ramp rats'.

Tony began his working life selling carpets for a living, but his family history drew him to Heathrow. He's not alone; Heathrow is full of people whose fathers, mothers or other family members work or worked at LHR. Given the strong family ties and Tony's length of experience at the airport, I felt it was probably wise to sit back and let him tell his story. Tony recalled:

> My dad worked for BEA. He started in 1966, worked in the cargo sheds. Started in the central area when the cargo was handled there, then moved to the southern airport

The Boeing 707 continued in use well into the jumbo jet era; this one was operated by Qantas. (*Richard Briggs*)

Loading and unloading at Terminal 2. (*Richard Briggs*)

cargo village when Terminal 1 was opened. He moved across to British Airways with the merger and finished with voluntary redundancy in 1980. My uncle also worked for British Eagle at LHR. Going from selling carpets was something of a career change, but BA is where I wanted to be. I did try my luck with the BAA, as it was then, but no joy. I started with BA cleaning cabins after everybody had left the aircraft after arrival, worked my way up to crew leader. We had a lot of fun too—most of the time anyway.

My team was cleaning a 747 and Harry Belafonte came back on board with a passenger services representative and asked if anyone had found his passport. He was sitting in first class so we went into first class to where he was sitting and his seat had already been done and re-dressed for the next departure, so I just asked the guy that was working that cabin and asked if he had found a passport; he said no, not seen anything. Belafonte asked if he was sure, and he did seem a little stressed. My guy confirmed he had not seen it, and with that Belafonte went into a tirade of abuse saying that we had stolen his passport. The passenger services rep tried to calm him down, but he wasn't having it. So I was getting annoyed with him and said if he was going to accuse me or any of my team then I want the police called and we can let them deal with this. He didn't want to take this course of action and left with the passenger service rep to see if the passport had been misplaced or was somewhere else. I didn't recognise him and it's was only my mate who said, 'Do you know who that was?' I said no and he said, 'That was Harry Belafonte...'

'Oh really?' was my reaction. We never heard any more so he must have found it. I had a close encounter with Madonna once too; it was in Terminal 4 and it was, I think, 1986 or '87. It was her first visit to the UK and she came in on Concorde and we were waiting for the passengers to get off the aircraft so that we could first raid the galley. That was always first priority with Concorde as the food was of better standard than the other aircraft and a free lunch is a free lunch. After that we had to clean the cabin, so we were waiting downstairs and there were lots of press trying to get pictures of her arrival so it was a little chaotic. We're always seeing celebrities come and go, especially now we're in T5 as the VIP area is close to ours.

The free lunch came only from food that was not consumed on the flight. The worst for this are the engineers, and they still are the worst; they can strip a galley clean in minutes, and get very irritated if anyone else is there. But otherwise all of the food is thrown away and any consumables that can be recycled will be.

It's the best job on the airport during the summer—worst in the winter. Rain you can deal with, with waterproof clothing, [but] the worst for me is a biting wind that seems to go right through you.

BA, like everybody else, did a lot of downsizing at one point, and the cabin cleaning work was outsourced so in 1991 they redeployed everybody around the airline and the airport. Downsizing usually means a lot of people being made redundant [and] it was a shock to most of us. It came about after the first Gulf War, when air travel declined and the airline went through cost-cutting measures and there were several parts of BA that were outsourced. There were people with families who thought they were out of a job, so it was a worrying time. I ended up in the [baggage] loading section in Terminal 1, which was a bit daunting as this department had just been shaken up ... there had been some issues with loaders opening passenger's bags and stealing items, so to go into this environment was a little bit scary, as were the rumours were that not all the ringleaders had been caught and new people were being targeted and were persuaded to join in the gangs that were operating in that department at the time. As with all rumours, this was not the case, but there was some pilfering going on. It was called 'dipping'.

In November 1983, the Brinks-Mat warehouse near Hatton cross was raided by a gang who departed with gold bars valued at £26 million. At the time, it was the biggest robbery in British history. By this point, Heathrow had gained something of a reputation for theft, with the tabloid newspapers dubbing it 'Thief-Row'. The police investigations into baggage theft failed to get anywhere, citing 'union problems'. Tony explained:

The union was very strong back then, but all union powers were whittled away over time. The union now is so weak that any changes to working conditions are just implemented. The strike of 1980 is still remembered by some of the old hands and mentioned even now from time to time are those who loaded bags during the strike. More recent is the cabin crew strike, and those ground crews who went to work for a short period onboard aircraft as cabin crew are still tagged as 'scabs'.

Union problems never hindered any investigation into dipping, it was trying to catch these guys, and in a small aircraft hold it is difficult to gather evidence. It was done in the end by mini cameras placed in the hold to record what went on. That was how the evidence was obtained, and most of the dippers were caught that way. Some did fall through the net and stayed at BA for some years, but it never got that bad again.

Back then when a new loader arrived, four-man teams were the norm for any flight. The new guy was always told to stay in the rest room. Then, later, perhaps the next day, an envelope would appear in your locker. Then you were told that was your share and to keep your mouth shut as you were involved now. If this was reported to the management then you were threatened, either in the car park on the way home or outside the rest room. Remember this was back in the late '70s, very early '80s, so CCTV and other surveillance equipment were not around.

I then became a crew leader again. I've probably loaded every aircraft type by now. We also loaded aircraft of other airlines that BA handled, and in 2004 I became a training officer and since then, [I] do as the job title says and train people to load airliners. On Site Demonstrator (OSD) and Crew Leader is the official title ...

It does have its lighter moments. Once a colleague and I were off-loading a cargo of gold bullion from a South African 747. We were sitting on a stack of gold bars trying to work out how much value it had. We stopped at $150 million...

There have been some high-profile incidents over the years but nobody has got away with it. This shipment was a normal thing from South Africa and it was left to ordinary loaders to deal with and the crew leader was briefed on what was on board. Once the hold doors were opened, the aircraft was surrounded by armed police officers who escorted the shipment, which was placed on two lorries and taken to the cargo terminal and then into London. While we waited for clearance to offload it, we were sitting on the stuff, which was placed in wooden boxes and sealed with metal restraining straps.

[They were] small boxes of about ten bars each; gold is heavy and there is a weight restriction on each pallet, so there were only six stacks of ten bars on each pallet.

Even allowing for occasions like sitting on gold, I had to ask Tony about his less enjoyable experiences of loading (Arctic winter winds and torrential rain apart). He told me that one of his low points was when his colleague and good friend was accused of drug-smuggling:

My friend was arrested and charged, went to trial and was acquitted. The ringleader got twenty-two years in prison I think. I had some customs people outside the house watching me for a few days after the arrest, and my bank account was looked at. At first I was angry, but it made sense for me to be looked at, if only to show I hadn't been involved—and of course I hadn't. Back then it was happening, and there was a small gang involved. This was at a time when a spate of robberies had happened.

At one time, New York JFK also had a shockingly bad reputation for cargo theft. It was mostly controlled by the mob—the cargo-theft scene in the movie *Goodfellas* was based on a true story at JFK. Just as matters have improved at Heathrow, so they have in New York, and many of those found guilty are now serving lengthy sentences in US prisons. Over recent years, a bigger issue has been Colombian drug-smuggling and Russian Mafia and Chinese Triad activity. It makes one wonder how bad it has been at Heathrow. I asked Tony whether drug-smuggling had ever been a real problem, or if there were ever any other issues over gang-related activity:

It was going on all the time back in the '90s. There was some gang involvement and it was organised. There was a TV documentary a few years ago about an airport worker who was running some of these gangs and then turned against them and informed customs. He turned super-grass because he got caught, but they never named him in the programme. But anyone who has worked for BA on the ramp knows who it was. He can't be named as he and his family are still in the witness-protection scheme.

My first thoughts after leaving school were about getting a job at Heathrow. As I was listening to Tony, I wondered how I might have reacted had I got a job at the airport. How would I have reacted had such approaches been made to me? If I had been approached by some gnarled, experienced baggage handler who was on the lookout for a cash-strapped young newbie, what would I have done? I would have refused to get involved, but I can understand why some were tempted.

Once the central area was complete, the size and shape of the airport was not altered for twenty years—aside from the extension of aircraft parking over withdrawn runways and the (constant) modification of the three terminals. However, Heathrow has changed almost beyond recognition over the past decade, and Tony has seen most of it:

Since I started there have been two new terminals—4 and 5, both of which I worked in. T4 was the first expansion out of the central area. I was still in cleaning at the time.

At T2's enlarged gates, east meets west; an Air Portugal 707 and an Aeroflot IL632. (*Richard Briggs*)

Same gates, different users; Iberia and Alitalia Boring 727s with an Air France A300. (*Richard Briggs*)

The whole operation was done overnight and all we did was move our vehicles and stores to a new base next to the Concorde stand at T4.

T5 opened in a blaze of publicity, but for the few weeks afterwards it was slated as a disaster. 'I could write a book myself about the T5 failures,' commented Tony, wryly.

Heathrow is not alone in having new terminal (or even new airport) problems. In the US, Stapleton Airport, Denver, like LHR and many other airports, had become restricted by encroaching development, so the City Authority found an alternative site miles away in the Colorado countryside. The new development was several times larger than Stapleton and comprised an expansive spread of runways and a massive terminal, and its reported cost was $2.66 billion.

It was due to open on 29 October 1993, but it didn't. Due to continuing problems with the baggage-handling system (among other issues), the opening was postponed from March until May, and then it was postponed again—and again. Its cost soared to $3.2 billion and continued to rise. Such were the delays and postponements that the airport's three-letter designator, DIA, took on new meanings; 'Delayed In Arrival' was one of the less offensive examples. DIA finally replaced Stapleton on 28 February 1995, sixteen months behind schedule and at a cost of $4.8 billion—nearly $2 billion over budget.

On the other hand, at least DIA eventually opened. Berlin's new airport still hasn't. Brandenburg International uses part of the site of the former East Berlin Airport at Schönefeld. The city's new, state-of-the-art airport expanded to the south, flattening the village of Diepensee in the process. Outwardly, at least, it has been structurally complete for some time; there are runways, taxiways, and a huge and impressive terminal, and yet none of them work.

The airport was originally planned to open in 2010, but the problems have been unending—baggage handling, the fire alarm system, take your pick. Project managers have been hired, fired, hired again, and fired again. Current estimates suggest that the airport could possibly open in 2018, or 2019 at the latest.

At Heathrow, T5 neared completion. Tony continued:

The way we were going to work was changing, and senior management thought this was a great opportunity to introduce new equipment and also a chance to get rid of any local agreements that the two terminals had had in T1 and T4. It was done too quickly. Because of the scale of the operation, a computer-based allocation system was being introduced. We had trialled this already on a small scale in T1, and it wasn't very successful on these trials … it was being forced through too fast.

In T5 we were training three months prior to the opening day, and there were also trials of the allocation system, but it wasn't a true trial as they were only picking a small proportion of the flights and not trying to see how the system would handle the whole operation. Needless to say, those of us who were trying to do the training could see what was going to happen and we warned our managers what we could see. They chose not to listen, thinking we were trying to ambush the operation. So when it went live on the opening day, the computer system was overloaded with demands just as we had warned it would be.

When T5 opened it was—is—a huge terminal (compared to T4 and T1) and we were going to have staff lost looking for their report point. All the interior corridors are all the same and you can think you're in one place but you're somewhere else. Also signage was poor, so as trainers we came up with a plan to have areas where people could get lost manned, so as to point people in the right direction—mobile signposts really. Again, management said this was not necessary as the hosting team who had done some of the familiarisation of the building could handle this. The only problem here was that they did not start until 6.30 a.m. on the first day and most of our staff needed to be in place and ready to go by 6.00....

We saw this as a bit of an error, so we had staff getting lost and a computer system that was not trialled correctly. It's not surprising it failed. Also, senior management were not informed by the middle management of our concerns and they were completely in the dark when it did fail. After the first two days of chaos, most of the middle-management team were nowhere to be seen by any higher managers, so it was left to the director level to take all the flak from the media and customers. That's why they could not answer any questions—because they were totally in the dark as to what happened.

After the first few days were over and some picture emerged as to how to get out of this mess, the senior management started to offer a two-for-one overtime rate for staff to sort all the bags and problems. Needless to say, it cost BA a small fortune to get back on track. If they had only listened to those who knew then it could have gone a lot smoother.

The problems in Denver and the ongoing saga in Berlin make T5's problems look a little less dramatic. As LHR has been in a constant state of flux, with changes an almost daily occurrence, one might wonder how resistant people are to what is really inevitable. Tony continued:

All the changes across the airport usually meet some resistance. You just get something settled and working, then along comes yet another change somewhere—but that's human nature. The change from a state-owned operator, as it was in the BAA days, to a privately owned operator, HAL, hasn't really affected me, although security is now much more of an issue. We have to jump through more hoops than we used to, and some of the people HAL employ seem to have got grumpier.

In order for Tony to train his students, someone has to train Tony. He explained:

We are trained on new equipment by the manufacturer. New aircraft—we get to use them first. The Airbus A380 is a good example. It was used on the Frankfurt route for familiarisation and we as an OSD team covered it every day and then passed on the knowledge to the rest of the crews when it went into service to Hong Kong. The reason for that is it was on the ground for a longer time.

T5 is BA's terminal but we also handle Iberia from T5. We handle any other aircraft that comes to T5. During the cabin crew strike back in 2010, we handled all the wet leased aircraft that BA used. Titan airways, jet 2, etc. We still have a small section in T3 for BA flights; they also handle some of the One World Group's flights as well.

There are several handling companies at Heathrow. DNATA, Menzies, and Servisair are three. The difference between them and us is they are separate companies to the airline and work on a contract basis, so they're cost-driven. BA, United and American employ their own staff ... and the airline's work has priority.

In Arthur Hailey's book *Airport*, the character of Joe Patroni says maintenance crews always help each other when needed, regardless of which company they work for. In real life, there is the example of a BA 747 that flew for a while with a South African Airways nose cone. I asked Tony what level of cooperation there was between the ground handling companies at Heathrow. He replied, 'We don't borrow anybody else's equipment, mainly because ours is generally in better condition than anybody else's.'

While there may not be much in the way of mutual aid in terms of ground equipment, Arthur Hailey got it right with the remark from Joe Patroni—especially in terms of safety. Airline management may well wish to cut the throats of their nearest competitor, but it's not uncommon to see airliners flying with parts borrowed from another airline—like the BA 747-436 with its grey and blue fuselage but white and orange nose.

Aircraft only make money when they are in the air, carrying people, so getting an airliner back into the air is a time-sensitive job. Tony remarked:

Currently we are under big pressure to get things done quickly. Sometimes even health and safety measures are overlooked....

Management will turn a blind eye if shortcuts are [taken], but if it goes wrong they will use that against anyone who breaks health-and-safety rules, because the management structure is built on bonuses—they are all trying to get their bonuses for the year, so [they] will look the other way when it suits them. Current turnaround time for an A319 is thirty-five minutes, A320 forty minutes, A321 forty-five minutes. All the long-haul types are a minimum of three hours to turn around.

There is an understated pride in Tony Horton—it is a feeling that despite the precarious nature of the airline industry, his job is still a good way to pay his taxes. Nevertheless, all airlines are always looking to cut costs, and Tony himself is now looking to leave:

There have been numerous occasions of redundancy throughout BA over the years, but it has never been an option for me until now, so I have decided to take an offer for voluntary redundancy that I hope will happen in the next few months. Over thirty years of doing shift work has taken its toll—my knees are giving me problems and the body can't take the work much longer. LHR and BA have been good to me over the past thirty years. It's enabled me to buy my house, which is very close to Heathrow, and to live and work in an environment that is fun and can be a challenge at times. I have met some very interesting people and have made many good friends who will always be good friends.

European airliners at Terminal 2 in the 1970s. (*Richard Briggs*)

The 707-336 lasted longer in British Airways service then the Rolls-Royce powered 436, but it was retired by 1984. (*Richard Briggs*)

7
Terminal 4

I first travelled the London–New York route with my dad, on the aforementioned BOAC Super VC10. For most people, it is the kind of trip that they will take just once in their lives—with the exception of the smart-suited businessmen (still wearing ties) and movie and TV stars, who flew on Concorde anyway. I've glided smoothly across the Atlantic (and occasionally bumped and bounced through CAT) numerous times, on four different types of aircraft—five, if you count the sub-types.

London to New York has a ring to it, but so does New York to Paris if you're a citizen of the US. For most Europeans, going to the USA is an event. For an American, doing it the other way round is an event for much the same reasons. Nevertheless, London–New York and New York–London has always been 'the' route to travel. Perhaps it's because New York has always been the traditional gateway to America—the city where Ellis Island, almost in the shadow of the Statue of Liberty, was once the point of entry. The island was superseded by JFK and its overcrowded International Arrivals Building. Those arriving at the city from overseas do so here, except if they have travelled by British Airways—the only non-US airline to still have its own facilities at JFK. TWA also had their own terminal, the Eero Saarinen-designed swooping vault that resembled an eagle rather than an airport passenger facility. Alternatively, one could fly Pan American to New York and use the airline's own Worldport terminal.

Real life has an unrelenting, remorseless, and irritating habit of getting in the way of one doing the things one really wants to do, so doing something for a living (and paying taxes) becomes necessary. However, when an opportunity comes along, it is often wise to take it. I found myself using T3 at Heathrow—the same terminal I had used years before (when it was called the Oceanic Building)—and scrambling eagerly on board Pan American's Boeing 747-121, registered in the USA as N732PA and named by Pan Am as *Clipper Ocean Telegraph*. Pan Am named all of their airliners, and all were prefixed by the '*Clipper*' title. The aircraft was the third Boeing 747 ever built, making its first flight on 10 July 1969. By March 1986 it was almost seventeen years old, and that's elderly for an aircraft. After it had been used by Boeing as part of the flight-testing programme, it was delivered to Pan Am on 13 July 1970, and the airline had been flying it ever since.

It was my first flight on a 747, even though the aircraft had been in service for nearly twenty years by this time. Most of my journeys had been around Europe with BEA, Air France, Lufthansa and other airlines. I had also flown via the RAF with my dad, to and from his postings on Cyprus. I had taken just one trip to the USA, years before, with my father—my small hand clutching his big one.

I had grown up looking skywards, watching the unmistakeable shape of Boeing's beast as it buzzed its way through the skies, the big fan-engines, as a rule, much quieter than the earlier screaming howl of the first-generation jets. I had read the public relations material, my youthful eyes absorbing stories of being able to go for a walk during those long flights, watching a movie, and being able to stretch out and relax in the wide open spaces of a roomy 747. In truth, absorbing or not, those PR stories were just that—stories. The first class lounge and bar behind the flight deck, in the hump on the forward fuselage, soon gave way to more seats as airlines discovered that a little judicious internal rearranging meant more seats could be installed up there. This, in turn, meant more revenue, and adding another row of seats here and there on the main deck had the same result. All airlines needed to maximise their incomes to pay for the huge debts they had run up acquiring fleets of 747s—Pan Am and British Airways included. The 747 that I boarded had therefore become a massive airborne bus.

Nevertheless, it was still my first time on the aircraft, so I subsumed myself in its size, which was still impressive by any standard. I watched as Heathrow's runway 09 Right slipped away. Ireland passed by. The movie was not particularly entertaining, and miles and miles of Atlantic Ocean don't give you much to look at either. North-east Canada passed by, then Boston, and then our descent began into New York. Our approach towards JFK was from the north and landing was on runway 22 right, which enabled a relatively short taxi to the Pan Am Worldport. The flight had taken seven hours and thirty minutes, much the same duration as that earlier journey on the BOAC Super VC10. The size of the 747 is dramatically enhanced when comparing it to the Boeing 727, one of which took me to my final destination—Dallas/Fort Worth—the next day. The 747 is a wide-bodied aircraft and the 727 is not, and difference is size is dramatic.

JFK is at its busiest in the late afternoon, when flights arrive from Europe, and in the evening, when they depart back across the Atlantic. Heathrow is busy all day, every day. I am not a fan of night travel, mostly because I don't get to see much when it's dark. I always ensure I have a window seat and a camera, even when flying at night. In daylight, there is always something to take a photograph of, even if it's just a passing cloud. Inevitably, however, my departure back to Heathrow three weeks later was at night, on board *Clipper Neptune's Car*. Still, dawn over the Atlantic was interesting, and an early morning arrival at LHR is when Heathrow is at its busiest for flights from the American continent. I was back at T3 again, which was crowded with British Airways 747s (and Concorde) and those from Pan Am, TWA, and a host of other long-haul airlines. All these routes were operated by wide-bodied aircraft, resulting in a lot of passengers crowding into the terminal. It was 4 April 1986, and half the throughput of T3 was about to vanish. Eight days after I arrived back from New York, Terminal 4 opened.

Only a few weeks before I had departed from T3 on Pan Am, a friend remarked, 'Not flying the flag?' after seeing my bright-blue-covered tickets for my transatlantic and US domestic Clipper excursions. My simple answer was that I had flown the flag innumerable times, even going back to the days of BOAC and BEA; it was time to try something I hadn't done before. I originally wanted to fly from Gatwick with Northwest since I had never used the Sussex airport, and Northwest were one of those latecomers crossing the Atlantic (along with Delta, American, People Express, and one or two others). This was in the days when airlines actually issued paper tickets; the colourful folders they came in became a collector's item for tax-deductible accountancy and the enthusiast.

Airlines also had their own ticket offices in those days, although cost-cutting and outsourcing has now seen most of them disappear. My visit to the Northwest ticket office was something of a let-down, and so were their computers—they couldn't issue anything, least of all a ticket, even to an eager wannabe like me. I tried TWA, but I wasn't very impressed by having a receptionist hand me a timetable and a typewritten list of fares when I wanted to sit down and discuss things. After all, I was still young, about to thrust myself on an unsuspecting world. I had not been on such a lengthy trip on my own before, and I wanted and needed advice. I thought perhaps they only gave advice to mature-looking and sober-suited businesspeople wearing ties, so I went to Pan Am, who styled themselves as 'The World's Most Experienced Airline'.

I was to go on a second trip across the pond less than three months after my Pan Am journey. This time, it was as much a question of convenience. When somebody says, 'Have this job, go get an air ticket and over here pronto,' one does. Since British Airways had a ticket office in my local high street and confirmation of an employment offer is not open-ended, convenience won the day. It also meant using the first terminal at Heathrow to be built outside the central area, and the first since T1 opened in 1968.

No new terminal had been built at Heathrow for eighteen years by the time T4 welcomed its first passengers, but the idea had been around for some time. The central area was packed to bursting and just three of the original six runways were still in use. Wide-bodied aircraft were in use even on shorter flights, so over 30 million passengers a year were using the three terminals. In 1983, in front of the early building work, the British Airports Authority put up what they believed was the world's largest free-standing sign, proudly proclaiming 'Terminal 4 opens in 1985'. The sign was quietly removed when 1985 became 1986.

Terminal 4 was a startling departure from the usual style of public buildings, especially of airports. This one had its guts unashamedly revealed, with exposed pipes and normally hidden entrails on show as the passengers entered. Running endlessly along the ceiling above one's head, almost nothing relieved the long row of check-in desks stretching out along the immediate interior. To find any semblance of airport lounges and shops, somewhere to eat and relax while waiting to soar aloft, one had to check in and then go through security. British Airways wanted sole use of the new terminal; the airline's chairman, Lord King, was still in the process of turning BA into a world-beater, but he had become used to getting his way. This time, however, he did not. BA were by far the dominant user, but they had to share the new terminal with KLM and Air Malta.

The ease with which passengers had been able to go to the right terminal had been eroded some time before T4's opening, as T1 had seen Israeli carrier El Al, Cyprus Airways, South African Airways, and Sabena (Belgium's national airline) move in alongside BA's flights to Miami and Chicago. These moves were required to ease the strain on both the other terminals. The opening of T4 and the transfer of all British Airways long-haul flights to the new terminal created something of a vacuum at T3, but the still steadily growing number of passengers rapidly filled the space left by the move. It also gave the BAA a chance to extensively refurbish T3.

Peter Masefield's quirky remark years before ('Alterations as usual during business') had turned out to be prophetic, and the airport has continued in this vein since. The T3 Departures building was extended towards the car park in front while normal operations continued, and the existing brick frontage was also replaced by a silvery skin that represented the space-age nature of air travel. The same style also was used on Terminal 2, while T1 retained its concrete look from the 1960s; there was no room to do anything else with it.

In June 1986, the still-new Terminal 4 looked and felt immense. It served a long row of BA 747s, most in the gleaming new paint scheme of pearl-grey upper fuselage and dark-blue lower fuselage, the tail fin now carrying the airline's proud crest and its serious slogan—'To Fly, To Serve'. Only Concorde retained the all-white fuselage, since paint doesn't work very well at supersonic speed, but it now also carried the airline's slogan on the fin. A rampant lion and an equally exuberant unicorn adorned the airline's crest; BA were on the rise, their advertising strap-line boldly proclaiming that they were 'the world's favourite airline' to all and sundry.

With two trips across the Atlantic quite close together, the comparison between a resurgent BA and a cash-strapped Pan Am was quite marked. BA were better on the ground, in the spanking new T4, and in the air, even though the aircraft were almost the same. They were both Boeing 747s, but Pan Am's now long-in-the-tooth 747-121 version was a stark contrast BA's fresh-looking and equally bulbous 747-2B4B.

Even though this BA-painted 747 looked outwardly and gloatingly identical to Pan Am's (apart from the colours), it was an updated version. Most of Pan Am's 747s were

The City of Lincoln awaits its passengers at Terminal 4 in June 1986. Directly behind and across runway 27 left/09 right is T3, and on the right are two Swissair Airbus A310s at T2. (*Author*)

delivered and placed into service in the early 1970s. The BA aircraft I boarded was actually owned by Middle East Airlines (MEA), based in Lebanon's capital, Beirut.

Beirut was being torn apart by war, and flying in and out of the airport there was only for the foolhardy as it was the scene of much of the fighting. MEA's solution to the conflict on the eastern coast of the Mediterranean was to lease out most of its aircraft—especially its fleet of high-value Boeing 747s, two of which were with BA in 1986. The British airline was in need of the extra capacity in order to handle the surge in passenger numbers they were experiencing. The aircraft were fully painted in BA's smart scheme and even registered in the UK for the duration of the lease—the one I flew on was G-BLVE, and MEA's aircraft are 747-200s.

The extra 'B' in my aircraft's name denoted that it was not only a -200 but a -200B— even more upgraded and improved over the earlier versions of the type, with this particular model having a large cargo door to the rear cabin. The only cargo it was carrying that day was the human kind, but its 'Combi' capability meant it retained the ability; the usual internal layout involves having passengers in the front half and cargo in the rear. When flying a passengers-only service, there is no sign of the cargo door inside the cabin.

Unlike Heathrow's brand-new Terminal 4, Chicago's O'Hare International Airport was a slightly different ball game. It was in the process of being rebuilt, with a new terminal rising for one of its two biggest airlines, United, and the other, American, about to get a complete refurbishment at its terminal. There was also a big and bright new terminal being planned for international carriers like BA, along with other foreign airlines that served the airport. Then, however, aircraft were parked out in the boondocks. Passengers had to go down an old-fashioned set of stairs from the aircraft and take a bus ride to a temporary terminal in a converted car park. It will be nice when it's all done.

It is the airport story writ large. Despite the downturn of the early 1970s, the numbers

Terminal 4, 1988. At one time, the departures approach road gave good views, including a close-up at its southern end. (*Author*)

of passengers and aircraft carrying them had continued to rise worldwide. The 1980s and into the 1990s saw new terminals and heavily refurbished terminals at most of the world's busiest airports. At the time O'Hare was the busiest airport in the world—but not in terms of solely international traffic. That honour remained back on the other side of the ocean, at Heathrow. Nevertheless, the scale of domestic operations—especially those of United and American—made O'Hare bustle like no other, all day, every day.

A week after I arrived, it was time to return to Heathrow, back aboard BA, with the flight being operated by the same aircraft that had been used on the outward journey. The dusk departure from O'Hare meant an early-morning arrival at the brand new T4. Away from the crowded central area, the ease with which one could use the brand-new facility made air travel more of a pleasure than it sometimes was.

Terminal 4's location gave air traffic controllers something to think about. Guiding arriving and departing aircraft to and from the runways and around the central area terminals was relatively straightforward, at least. T4 is on the southern edge of the airport, and located south of runway 5—or 27 left/09 right, if you prefer.

In order to give some relief to residents, two runways are predominantly used—one for departures and one for arrivals. At 3 p.m. every day, the runways switch around. This means that aircraft departing from T4 have to cross an active runway if 27 left, the southern runway, is being used for arrivals; this can cause delays. At its busiest (which is most of the time), aircraft arrive at Heathrow every ninety seconds, so it doesn't leave a lot of time for a 747 to get across the runway. There might even be an element of danger to the practice, but LHR's ground controllers are adept and capable, as are BA's pilots.

Terminal 4 was a success from the day it opened. For British Airways, it gave a boost to the airline's efforts to shed its 1970s, state-owned image, turning it from a dowdy institution into what it claimed to be—the world's favourite airline.

Taken from the northern end of Terminal 4's approach road, looking towards the threshold of runway 27 left. (*Author*)

8
Big Blue and White

The desire to reach for the sky runs deep in our human psyche.

Cesar Pelli

The vast majority of people don't travel much. Some people travel a lot and see a big chunk of the world, others may circumnavigate the world and see all of it, and others may never go beyond the borders of the town where they are born, grow up, live, work, and ultimately pass on to the next world.

The legendary founder and chairman of Pan American World Airways, Juan Trippe, was one of those who had the background and connections to travel. He also had vision. That vision saw him build Pan Am into a globe-encircling giant—a company that, at its height, allegedly held more influence than the local US consulate. It was fitting that the same vision saw Juan Trippe sign the launch order for the Boeing 747, an airliner twice the size of the biggest then in service. The 747's single greatest asset was its ability to carry sufficient people economically enough to bring air travel within the reach of almost anybody, and it was Pan American who were at the forefront of it—like they always had been. As early as 1943, Trippe had said:

> Air Transport has a very clear choice; of becoming a luxury service to carry the well-to-do at high prices, or to carry the average man at what he can afford to pay.

Pan Am had grown up in a world in which everything had a place and everything was in its place. It was a world in which airlines flew on routes that were set in a framework that enabled them to have a near monopoly on what they did. Even so, there was still some competition; if you wanted to fly from London Heathrow to New York, you could choose from four airlines—two US-based ones and two British-based ones. The trouble was they had a tendency to offer similar fares and similar service because no other airline was allowed to operate scheduled services on the route.

The two US carriers were Pan Am and TWA. The British, however, controlled their airline industry even more than the US authorities; only BOAC and subsequently British Airways were allowed to serve long-haul routes. This left an opening for anybody who had the cash to start an airline, overcome the objections of BOAC/BA and successive UK governments, and run a viable service from London to New York. Attempts to fill that opening had been made by various companies over the years, from British Eagle to Laker Airways and British Caledonian. Some lasted longer than others, but all ultimately failed. It took the appearance of Virgin Atlantic, with its charismatic founder Richard Branson, for a second UK-based airline to succeed. Even so, in 2015, Virgin celebrated the thirtieth anniversary of their first flight by losing a lot of money, dropping some routes, and going into partnership with Delta in a bid to get out of the red and back into profit. This was despite them having been BA's primary international competitor longer than anyone else. When the peaks are high, the money that comes in is mind-boggling. The lows can be equally stunning, and, in some cases, company-shattering.

Two things changed much of the above. The 747's economics was one factor, and the other was an event in November 1978—the US Airline Deregulation Act, which changed what had been a well-ordered marketplace into something akin to a Turkish bazaar on a bad day. With the passing of the act, any American air carrier could fly any route and charge any fare.

The only exception was Pan Am. Their biggest rivals, TWA, already had a viable domestic network to feed passengers into the international routes from JFK, including Heathrow. Pan American World Airways was a long-distance carrier, as its name implied, and it had always irritated Juan Trippe not only that Pan Am had no domestic feed, but also that anyone who chose to travel with his airline from New York had to change both airlines and terminals at JFK. The design of JFK's central terminal area (the CTA) had never made that easy—it was time-consuming and inconvenient. It was even more difficult than at Heathrow; for its first forty years, Heathrow had just three terminals,

US rivals Trans World Airlines (TWA) never quite reached the same scale as Pan Am. (*Richard Briggs*)

Pan Am slightly revised their livery in 1976, with larger titles and the swirling 'Clipper' name. The design was starkly illustrated worldwide twelve years later. (*Richard Briggs*)

Pan Am's Heathrow operations were big enough to warrant their own ground handling, as demonstrated by the blue vans as a 747-121 is refuelled on a remote stand. (*Richard Briggs*)

whereas JFK had nine. This was a problem that TWA didn't have since they also had their own terminal serving both domestic and international routes.

There was now also another problem at JFK. The same orderly methods that had served Pan Am well over the years—namely that people would cross the Atlantic via primary hubs like New York—were now being eroded by both US and foreign airlines who were serving secondary destinations directly. This also impacted on TWA; why fly from Dallas to New York, change planes (albeit in the same terminal), and then go on to Europe when you could fly direct with American Airlines? Then again, who in their right mind would fly with a domestic airline from anywhere in the USA to JFK and then have to navigate the intricacies of the CTA layout before catching a Pan Am flight across the ocean?

Juan Trippe retired in 1968 after committing his airline to buying twenty-five 747s and providing the means to operate them, which represented a heavy expense—not least the expansion of the airline's JFK terminal, the Pan American Worldport. It was left to his successors to try and steer the airline through the trials and tribulations of the next decades. There are many differing opinions and thousands of words written about the wisdom (or lack of it) behind the decisions of Pan Am's leadership following Trippe's departure, but most people saw only what happened when flying with the airline.

At the beginning of December 1988 I made my second journey from Heathrow to the Pan Am Worldport. I was on board N9670 *Clipper Empress of the Skies*, a 747-123 delivered originally to American Airlines. Like all of Pan Am's aircraft, it was a relatively old airliner, and it looked it. Despite being painted in the 'new' livery, with the big billboard titles on the side, it was dirty and looked generally unkempt.

December 1988. (*Author*)

Terminal 3 on a misty day on December 1988. (*Author*)

The service on board was average—not bad, by any means, but not especially outstanding either. One good point was the cabin walk-round by the captain midway across the Atlantic. I would remember his face three weeks later.

The flight was at least on time, and it arrived at JFK in clear-blue skies and bright sunlight. I had a couple of hours to fill, so I spent the time at the same vantage point as on my previous visit, at the far end of the Worldport, taking photographs of the comings and goings from the long bay runway directly in front of it. The sun went down. I took more pictures, including those of Delta Airlines arrivals and departures from the terminal next to the Worldport, originally built for Northwest and Braniff Airways.

Delays were common, and my flight wasn't going anywhere soon. Eventually the flight boarded, and we sat some more. The delays were not improving. We did go eventually, and despite the late departure I made my connecting flight at Dallas/Fort Worth to Austin—although only just. The aircraft used from New York, the ubiquitous Boeing 727 (this one a -227), carried an apt name: *Clipper Flying Eagle*. Yes, you are right—the 727 was not originally delivered to Pan Am, whose Boeing customer number was 21. The aircraftr was orignally delivered to Braniff Airways fourteen years earlier.

My business done, I was back at the Worldport just over a week later for a late-evening departure to London, peering at the brightly lit ramp through the windows at *Clipper Champion of the Seas*, N734PA, another of Pan Am's original 747s. Things were moving more smoothly this time.

An on time departure, a smooth flight through the night, on time into Heathrow and I'm home. Two weeks later, everything changed.

9
One Night, One Flash of Light

Perhaps travel cannot prevent bigotry, but by demonstrating that all peoples cry, laugh,
eat and die, it can introduce the idea that if we try and understand each other, we may
even become friends.

Maya Angelou

For the most part, planes criss-cross the skies almost incessantly—yet we never see them and
we never hear them. They are too high up, too far above us for anyone to even glance unless
accidentally, the result of a momentary look upwards and a glimpse of a long, thin, white
vapour trail left by the engines of transatlantic airliners coming and going from Europe to the
Americas or *vice versa*. Most of them funnel along the air corridors above the United Kingdom.

The sky is never as empty as it sometimes seems. At one time, I lived not too far from
Heathrow, and most departures would soar over my part of town, low enough for me to see
the colours of the aircraft and know which airline it was serving. Come to that, they were low
enough to be heard—especially Concorde, whose distinctive sound became apparent shortly
after take-off before growing to a peak and then fading as it headed west to New York.

All aircraft keep to pre-planned routes along the equivalent of highways in the sky, and
even airliners whose journeys start in the Middle East and southern and central Europe
all use the same part of those aerial roads, the ones that cross England, Wales, Scotland
and Ireland. The traffic is joined by departures and arrivals from UK-based airports like
London, Manchester, and Glasgow. It's the ones that have come from elsewhere, the
ones just passing by, that leave the vapour trails above the UK skies. At night, if you care
to look, the flashing lights of aircraft appear like moving stars against the deep blue of
space, the vapour trail invisible—unless it's cloudy, when you don't see or hear anything.

This is true until the unthinkable becomes reality.

It was my dad who told me. It was December 1988 and I was upstairs, tinkering
around with my model aircraft, when he came leaping up and said, 'A Pan Am Boeing
747 has crashed in Scotland.'

He had heard it on the radio; as a retired radio broadcaster, my father always had a radio
on. That night, however, we were both glued to the TV news. Images of burning houses
and flames leaping high into the dark night are still etched into my mind even now, over
twenty-eight years later. So are the images that appeared over the next few days; the huge

crater amongst the shattered homes in a devastated Scottish town, seats, personal belongings, and twisted, broken metal in the streets of a place few had ever heard of. Then, curiously, there was the way in which the entire nose section had landed in a field almost by itself, some considerable distance from the main part of the devastation, and still seemingly in one piece. It was a little misshapen, but it was instantly recognisable as a Boeing 747, the thin blue line across the cabin windows and the swirling script of the name—*Clipper Maid of the Seas*.

Airliners occasionally crash; it's one of the more unpalatable facts of life. When they do, people sometimes die, and if they do, it's often in large numbers. This is why it's deemed so newsworthy, even though more people die in road accidents and at home, where one tends to feel safe. It's actually very rare for airliners to crash, so when they do it's big news—often reported inaccurately, as the headline matters more than the facts.

As the days passed and more images emerged, the blame game started—most of it aimed at Pan Am itself. There were stories about the American Federal Aviation Authority (FAA) issuing fines for safety violations, but the safety violations by American air carriers are rarely, if ever, anything either mechanical or related to the aircraft itself, or the procedures used by the airline to maintain them. Instead, most are for things like missing or worn stickers on the back of seats (the ones that say 'your life vest is under your seat) or a malfunctioning toilet-engaged sign. There was also wild speculation about old 747s that should have been put out to pasture years ago—accusations that the cash-strapped Pan Am were cutting corners on aircraft maintenance.

There were many shocking images, but it always came back to the striking picture of the nose of *Clipper Maid of the Seas*, lying on its side on a patch of damp earth. It was instantly recognisable. To many people in the UK and around the world, what was not recognisable was the name of the place where the crash had occurred—a small town sitting underneath the aerial road, living in relative anonymity until one awful night. It is a place whose name is now written into tragic history; Lockerbie.

Even today, the very mention of the town evokes memories of that night. There are few tragedies (at least in the UK) that are as instantly recognisable whenever they are mentioned. Hungerford, where a lunatic ran amok with guns, is another—the town is a tiny place some way to the west of London and not too far from Heathrow. However, Lockerbie stands apart, and whenever it is mentioned, the image of the nose of the 747 comes to mind. On newspapers or TV, the image is always the same. It is as if that one picture encapsulates everything about that fateful night, and of the company that once stood for everything that was good about air travel.

In the frenzy of both broadcast and print-media coverage in those first few days afterwards, it seemed to occur to nobody that the entire front end of a 747 doesn't just drop off for no reason, leaving the rest of the aircraft to fall to the ground. As the grieving gathered at the Worldport, waiting for news of the flight that wasn't coming home, I have no doubt that Pan Am's ground staff were handling it with the utmost professionalism and respect, outwardly showing no feelings other than empathy with those waiting. Inside their very souls, what were they feeling? I had been in the Worldport just two weeks before, and I remember the palpable pride of the gate agent who had told me Pan Am were taking over the terminal next door to the Worldport for the airline's domestic services. I remember the friendliness of the ground crew taking advantage of a quiet few moments with me as I watched and photographed arriving and departing aircraft on the bay runway at the far end of the Worldport's 747 extension. I remember how we watched as a company Airbus A310, caught by the wind, wobbled as it neared the long strip of concrete. 'Bring it on home,' murmured the Pan Am lady sitting next to me, as if willing her colleagues a safe and gentle touchdown. It was. I remember their encouragement and enquiries as to whether or not I got the picture right when my shutter clicked and I lowered the camera. I thought not only of the relatives and friends of the crew and passengers on board *Clipper Maid of the Seas*, but also of the Pan Am staff at the Worldport and elsewhere in the US. For that matter, I thought of the Pan Am staff at Heathrow, from where *Clipper Maid of the Seas* had departed not long before it came down.

What were they feeling? They had lost their own, and they were experiencing the same media coverage as everyone else.

Was it really the airline's fault? In June 1985, Air India Boeing 747 VT-EFO, named *Emperor Kanishka*, disappeared into the Atlantic Ocean on its way from Canada to Heathrow, the first leg of its journey back to New Delhi and Bombay. At almost the same time, in Tokyo, 6,000 miles away, Canadian Pacific Airlines flight 003 had arrived from Vancouver and had been unloaded, with the passenger's bags now below the terminal and being readied for collection. At 3.20 p.m. local time, one bag exploded. The flight had arrived early. Had it been on time or late, there would have been a terrible disaster; there was no doubt that the force of the explosion would have been powerful enough to cause the destruction of the Canadian-operated 747 used for the flight.

The weather over the Atlantic following the disappearance of *Emperor Kanishka* was unusually kind, even for mid-summer, allowing for a painstaking search to find and map the wreckage on the sea bed. In a remarkable achievement, the flight data and cockpit voice recorders were recovered along with a substantial amount of the aircraft's remains. The investigation revealed that whatever had brought the 747 down had been sudden and catastrophic, with no warning and no chance for the crew to react. In August, less than two months after the crash of the Air India flight, a Japan Air Lines 747 departed Tokyo Haneda Airport on a domestic flight to Osaka. Less than fifteen minutes after

Air India, who fly between the UK and India but also between the UK and New York. (*Richard Briggs*)

take-off, something went seriously wrong. The flight crew reported a complete loss of control of the aircraft, and despite heroic efforts on their part, the aircraft crashed into Mount Osutaka with the loss of 520 of the 524 on board.

The summer of 1985 had become one of the worst in commercial aviation history. In less than two months, two Boeing 747s had mysteriously crashed, killing 849 people. Both aircraft had apparently suffered some kind of sudden failure. At that time, 610 Boeing 747s were being operated by sixty-nine airlines around the world. If the 747 was inexplicably suffering from some kind of structural problem, answers would have to be found quickly.

Back in Canada and Japan, painstaking investigations had revealed that an Indian terrorist group was responsible for the explosion in Tokyo. Due to political unrest in India, it was increasingly likely that the same group had been responsible for planting a bomb on the Air India flight. However, most of the wreckage of the *Kanishka* still lay on the seabed of the Atlantic, and what had been recovered so far did not indicate a bomb. The JAL 747 did at least have wreckage to examine, even though it was in a difficult site to get to. The day after the crash, parts of the fin and rudder, along with other parts of the rear of the aircraft, were found floating in Sagami Bay. It was discovered that almost half of the tail fin had detached in flight.

As the investigation proceeded, an inspection of the aircraft's history revealed that it had suffered a tail scrape during a landing in 1978, and Boeing engineers had been called in to repair damage to the rear pressure bulkhead. Photographs of the Air India wreckage were examined to see if there was a link, but the bulkhead was found to be intact.

After much intensive footslogging and working with the Japanese Police, the Canadian investigators had found that the Tokyo airport explosion had been the result of a bomb hidden inside a Sanyo stereo tuner. Records in Japan showed that 2,000 units had been shipped to Canada, and they were even able to identify the store that had sold it.

In Japan, the investigation into the JAL crash had reached a satisfactory conclusion. In an admirably open and honest move, Boeing admitted that the rear bulkhead had been incorrectly repaired after the earlier incident involving the 747. When the aircraft took off on its fateful flight, the bulkhead had ruptured, causing the fin to disintegrate and severing power lines to the controls in the cockpit.

The investigation's conclusion ended any link between to two disasters. As suspicions of a bomb on board the Air India flight mounted, the integrity of the world's 747 fleets was upheld. The Canadian Air Safety Board (CASB) report released in January 1986 supported the bomb theory, although it conceded that there could not be certainty. It stated:

> There is considerable circumstantial and other evidence to indicate the initial event was an explosion occurring in the forward cargo compartment. This evidence is not conclusive. However, the evidence does not support any other conclusion.

There was clearly a precedent for airliner bombings, so why were so many so quickly inclined to put the blame for Lockerbie on Pan Am? Much of that blame was apportioned to the airline's own security arrangements. When I checked in for my flight to New York at the beginning of December 1988, I was questioned as to the contents of my bags. Were they mine? Yes. Had I packed them myself? Yes. Had I been given anything to take by anybody else? No.

Other than physically opening my bags and having their contents looked at, I'm not sure what else could be done, apart from x-raying everything. I don't know if that was done; I am a passenger, not an expert in such matters. However, I do know that the security of a flight is not and should not be the sole responsibility of an airline. An airline's job is to carry people from one place to another, flying the aircraft safely, in reasonable comfort, and (if possible) in a timely manner.

An airline's aircraft sits on the ground for some time in between flights. During that time, it is accessed by a number of people, often employed by different companies. In days gone by, airlines employed their own cleaners and their own caterers—in fact, pretty much everybody who had anything to do with turning around an airliner between flights was employed directly by the airline concerned. For many airlines, those days ended years before *Emperor Kanishka* and *Clipper Maid of the Seas* came down. Economic reality kicks in, and it's the same for all airlines; by the 1980s, they were concentrating on their core function of transporting people from A to B, Pan Am included.

Unlike *Emperor Kanishka*, the wreckage of *Clipper Maid of the Seas* was strikingly accessible. The painstaking and lengthy investigation was able to prove that a bomb hidden in a bag in the forward cargo compartment (just as in the Air India bombing) had brought the aircraft plummeting onto Lockerbie. The investigators were even able to prove when and where the bomb had begun its journey. Its well-documented passage began at Malta, on board a flight to Frankfurt, before it was loaded onto another flight to London. It was finally loaded onto the Pan Am 747 at Heathrow. Nevertheless, there are still doubts; is it possible that what has been made public is not entirely true, or not true at all? For example, is it possible that the bomb was loaded onto *Clipper Maid of the Seas* by a 'sleeper' agent—someone who does a regular day-to-day job like loading bags onto a plane until the time comes for them to be activated? Anything is possible. No terrorist group ever claimed responsibility for the bombing of the Air India flight. Although some spurious claims were made, no terrorist group ever claimed credible responsibility for Lockerbie either.

The responsibility was apportioned to Libya and its then-leader Muammar Gaddafi. The one person convicted of the act itself was the now-deceased Abdelbaset al-Megrahi, who persistently maintained his innocence. Was al-Megrahi a convenient fall guy? The answer is unclear, and it's unlikely that the truth will ever come entirely out. Several years later, when a TWA 747 crashed into the Atlantic shortly after departing from JFK, there was a general feeling of sympathy towards the airline on both sides of the ocean. Numerous theories have been put forward (and some quite vehemently), none of which blamed the airline. This didn't ultimately prevent TWA from being absorbed by American Airlines as TWA's own financial problems overcame them. No such sympathy seemed to extend towards Pan Am, but Pan Am did not place a bomb on its aircraft.

In the end, the responsibility lies with the person or persons still unknown. Al-Megrahi couldn't have done it all by himself, packing the explosives and ensuring they went onto the right flight at the right time and in the right place.

Lockerbie was a tragedy in every sense of the word. From a purely personal point of view, and probably a selfish one, the loss extends to me. I had what could be termed as a narrow escape; if the plan had been executed three weeks earlier, I would have been one of those on board. When photographs of *Clipper Maid of the Sea*'s pilot in command,

Captain James MacQuarrie, were released, I recognised the face as the same captain who had taken the time to do a walk around the cabin and talk to the passengers on board my flight from Heathrow to the Worldport at the start of December 1988.

I grew up with Pan American World Airways, amongst others, as an aviation enthusiast. It took a long time to actually fly with them, but when I did, I flew with history. They struggled on for another three years; had Lockerbie not happened, it's possible they might have survived. Thomas Plaskett, appointed as Chairman of Pan Am earlier in the year, seemed to be heading the airline in the right direction, and morale amongst the employees was rising.

Lockerbie sucked the life out of the company. Pan American—big blue and white, New York's most dominant airline and one of the biggest players at Heathrow—closed down for good on 4 December 1991, ending sixty years of pioneering aviation history. Its New York JFK terminal, the Worldport, passed to Delta Airlines, who replaced Pan Am as JFK's biggest airline. At the end of 2013, the terminal was demolished.

No trace of Pan Am now remains, either at JFK or Heathrow.

Two months after the 1986 Canadian report into the Air India explosion, I boarded *Clipper Ocean Telegraph* and flew to the Worldport on my first trip aboard a Boeing 747. Three weeks later, I returned to London on board *Clipper Neptune's Car*, another 747. Two and a half years later, I repeated the same journey, on *Clipper Empress of the Skies*, to New York, and then back to London on board *Clipper Champion of the Seas*.

All these flights were safe. Pan Am flew me all around the USA—safely. Just two weeks after my last flight with them, flight PA103, operated by *Clipper Maid of the Seas*, departed from London Heathrow.

The Air India flight was running late. Had it been on time, the flight may well have been over the UK when the bomb detonated. *Clipper Maid of the Seas* departed late. Had it been on time, the bomb would have exploded over the Atlantic.

To date, the atrocity that was Lockerbie remains the deadliest aviation incident, as well as the deadliest act of terrorism, to occur in the United Kingdom.

At their peak, Pan American were one of Heathrow's biggest operators. (*Richard Briggs*)

10

Tearing Metal

Now he has departed from this strange world a little ahead of me...

Albert Einstein

Heathrow is one of the safest airports in the world. The same can be said for UK airspace and UK airlines. The accident record for all three is one of the very best. That record of transporting people from one place to another without injuring or killing them is a testimony to the people whose job it is to make air travel as safe as it is. Still, accidents do happen. There are airports that have had safety records that make flying into them (and, for that matter, out of them) more interesting.

Regardless of aircraft type, the two most dangerous parts of any airborne excursion are take-off and landing. Few accidents happen while *en route*, outside of mid-air collisions or sabotage. Aircraft have been known to crash because they take off too steeply and thus stall, or had their flaps incorrectly set or retracted too early. An example would be the 1972 Trident crash at Staines, which came down just after departing from Heathrow. Other crashes have involved aircraft descending too rapidly and hitting the ground before reaching the airport. This is euphemistically known as 'controlled flight into terrain', a term also applied to flying into mountains.

Thankfully, wind shear is almost unknown at Heathrow. This is when a change in wind speed and/or direction within a short distance results in a tearing or 'shearing' effect (hence the name). Wind shear has been known to occur in both a horizontal and a vertical direction, and occasionally in both. Think of it like this; it's a windy and rainy day, so you will probably use an umbrella to at least keep your upper half dry, although not necessarily your legs. Most people will angle the umbrella to shield the user from the wind. This is fine until the wind apparently changes its often-unpredictable mind and comes at you from another direction, or seemingly several directions at the same time, without warning—which is why umbrellas are notorious for being blown inside-out, a near-perfect demonstration of wind shear for the pedestrian.

The year 1985 was not a good one for commercial aviation. As well as the loss of Air India's 747 *Emperor Kanishka* over the Atlantic and the Japan Air Lines 747, the third major incident that month occurred nearer to home, at Manchester's Ringway (MAN) Airport. A Boeing 737-236 of British Airtours experienced a major failure of the port (left) engine during its take-off run and while still on the runway. The failure ignited the fuel carried in the wing, unknown to the cockpit crew, who had only an engine failure alert in the cockpit. They acted entirely correctly, aborting the take off and turning off the runway, to the right, stopping the aircraft on the runway-to-taxiway turn-off.

Aircraft take off and land into the wind—at least as far as possible. Crosswinds are okay up to a point, but aircraft don't like tailwinds. It has always been this way. Tailwinds are when wind blows into the rear of a landing or departing aircraft, and they are avoided where possible. It is ideal to have wind blowing directly along the runway, towards the aircraft—except in the case of the 737 at Manchester. There, the wind blew the flames from the burning left wing (now directly facing the wind) onto the fuselage, destroying the rear of the aircraft. Eighty-four people got out by using the escape routes on the right-hand side of the aircraft, away from the flames. Fifty-four died, despite the aircraft never leaving the ground.

Had the wind been blowing from the other direction, Manchester's taxiway, parallel to the single runway the airport had at the time, would have been on the left, not the right. The aircraft would thus have turned to its left to leave the runway, and the burning fuel would not have been blown back onto the aircraft. Since this accident, standard procedures have been changed; an engine failure alert now requires air crew to stay on the runway after stopping the plane and turn it with the failed engine away from the wind.

Unlike so many other aspects of life, in commercial aviation lessons are usually learned from tragedy. However, accidents can still happen, and often for very different reasons. As rare as they are, they can even occur in the United Kingdom and, like Manchester, Heathrow has seen some of them. It has been the point of departure for a flight that never reached its supposed destination—like *Clipper Maid of the Seas*. It has also been the intended point of arrival for a flight that never made it, as it was for the *Emperor Kanishka*.

British Airways has a proud and long history. By any measure, British Airways and its predecessors, BOAC and BEA, are as good as any and better than most, and today British Airways are one of the safest airlines in the world, as they always have been. As Heathrow's biggest user, its aircraft depart and arrive incessantly every day. One of them, Boeing 777-236 G-YMMM did, in fact, arrive, but not as smoothly as normal.

At the time of writing, it is Heathrow's most recent incident. At the critical moment on final approach towards the Great West Road and the threshold of runway 27 left, both the aircraft's engines lost power. Thanks to the skill of the crew, the flight skimmed the perimeter fence; with no engine thrust to keep it in the air, the 777 landed on the grass, its main wheels breaking off, before sliding to a halt right on the runway's threshold markings. Nobody died. The aircraft was seriously damaged to the extent that it had to be written off, but all on board walked away.

Heathrow has seen its share of aborted take-offs, tricky landings, and emergencies. However, you have to go back to 1968 to find the last accident that resulted in the loss of an aircraft. In April, BOAC flight BA712, a Boeing 707-465 registered as G-ARWE (one of two originally destined for the ultimately unsuccessful British Eagle Airways, hence the Boeing customer number), departed for Sydney and one engine exploded, resulting in the power plant falling away from the aircraft and landing in a disused gravel pit near Thorpe. With the wing now on fire, the crew made an immediate return to Heathrow, landing on Runway No. 2 and coming to a blazing halt directly in front of spectators on T2's roof gardens. All bar five of those on board escaped before the aircraft was almost completely destroyed by the flames.

In July of the same year, an arriving BKS Airspeed Ambassador freighter aircraft suffered a control rod failure, causing one wing to drop and hit the ground. The aircraft careered into Terminal One's aircraft-parking area, ripping off the tail of a BEA Trident 1 and coming to rest after slicing a second BEA Trident in half. Since then, there were no major catastrophes within the perimeter of Heathrow until the BA 777 crash-landing.

According to statistics from the International Air Transport Association (IATA), 2014 was the safest year ever for air transport, with the number of fatal accidents at a record low when compared with the number of flights. The IATA's annual safety report states that 641 people died in airline accidents. Although this figure includes the 239 people on board Malaysian Airlines flight 370—which is still, at the time of writing, missing somewhere in between Kuala Lumpur and its destination, Beijing—it does not include those who died on Malaysian Airlines flight MH17, which was shot down over Ukraine, since this was clearly not an accident. It may sound like a lot, by 641 deaths compared to the death toll on any country's roads is a small number. The fact remains that the chances of being killed or injured in a car on the way to or from an airport are much higher than in a commercial airliner on any airline.

Although there have occasionally been minor incidents and emergency landings, Heathrow remains one of the world's safest airports.

Terminal 2 in 1985. (*Author*)

The roof gardens had become smaller by 1985, but they still provided a good view. (*Author*)

Above: A number of airlines introduced new colour schemes in the mid-1980s, some after experimenting with variations of their existing styles, like SAS, as shown on this DC9. (*Author*)

Below: The highest floor of the car park next to Terminal 2 offered reasonable views of runway 27 left/09 right and the taxiway along side it. (*Author*)

A TriStar departure seen from the roof gardens in 1985. (*Author*)

A view from the car park's top floor in 1988; a Swissair A310 departs. (*Author*)

The view from what was a public seating area in Terminal 1. (*Author*)

BA's Tridents had long gone by 1988, replaced by the Boeing 737 (left), but the BAC111s soldiered on with hush-kitted engines. Within three years, TWA's 747s would also disappear from Heathrow. (*Author*)

A Heathrow landmark is visible just behind the landing Cyprus Airways A310—the Southall gasometer. It still has the code 'LHR' painted on it to help pilots tell the difference between Heathrow and RAF Northolt, which lies only a few miles north of the airport. (*Author*)

An Air Canada L1011 TriStar is leaving while a KLM Boeing 737 arrives. (*Author*)

11
Dead Man's Shoes II

*The modern airplane creates a new geographical dimension. There are no distant places
any longer: the world is small and the world is one.*

Wendell Willkie

In May 1997, three months short of his birthday, thirteen-year-old Neil Martin went to
bed early, set his alarm, got up early, and rode his bike from his home in Bedfont, a few
miles south of Heathrow, past the Green Man pub and to the Great South West Road.
Then he watched the hangar that had housed Concorde get blown up.

The hangar had originally been built along with the rest of the BOAC maintenance
area back in the 1950s, and it was built to last. This made it very difficult to demolish
when it was no longer needed, so it was blown up. It was intended to be a controlled
bang, and one that should have brought the building down in the same way that tower
blocks and factory chimneys are brought down, with no toppling sideways and no impact
on those nearby. However, this one did impact on those living close to the airport and
also further away—loudly. According to newspaper reports at the time, 'the contractors
had promised the authorities at London's Heathrow airport that the demolition of an
old aircraft hangar would be inaudible'. The explosion was heard up to 7 miles away,
and local residents thought the airport had been attacked by terrorists. The demise of
Concorde's hangar was the end of one era but the continuation of another.

Neil now works at Heathrow, scaring birds and marshalling aircraft, amongst other
things—he's a Senior Airfield Safety Officer, and he's the third generation of the Martin
family to have worked at the airport. In 1949, Neil's grandfather, Michael (more often
known as 'Micky'), joined BEA at Northolt, working for BEA's Cargo division. He
transferred to Heathrow with the airline after its operations moved to their new home
in the central area. At the same time as the airport was being built, houses were being
built nearby—all within easy distance of the burgeoning airport. Most were aimed at
providing homes for the army of people who would work there. Micky Martin was
one. Did any of them know how noisy it was going to get? Was noise ever a real issue?
One suspects not. Most of the houses around Heathrow today are still occupied by
people who directly or indirectly earn their livelihood from being close to the airport.
The protests and complaints often come from those who actually live further away—
sometimes in bigger houses, with bigger incomes—and use Heathrow to go away on

business and holiday. Bedfont, east and west, lies south of the airport, less than the distance of Heathrow's two remaining runways. BEA themselves built a number of the homes that airport people moved into, with street names reflecting their origin—Ensign Road, Viscount Way and Argosy Lane. Micky and his wife watched theirs being built.

When the new cargo area on the southern edge of Heathrow opened, Micky moved across to work there, the ramp being filled with the eye-catching twin-boomed Argosy freighter, one of which carried the car from the 1960s movie *Chitty Chitty Bang Bang* to Austria for its on-location filming. With the withdrawal of the Argosy, the 'Merchantman', as BEA called the converted Vanguard passenger type, came into freighter service, having been relegated from carrying people like me from Jersey to Heathrow—1974, one of the last passenger flights of the Vanguard.

The never-ending building work meant it was almost inevitable that things would occasionally not work as they should. In 1970, an East German Ilyushin IL18 made a rare visit to Heathrow operated by the country's flag-carrier, Interflug. The aircraft arrived to collect a cargo of barrels of antifreeze, but the barrels were found to be missing; it was subsequently discovered that they had been bricked in behind a new wall. Lufthansa were Interflug's West German counterpart, and they became the only German flag-carrier (although not the only German airline) as Interflug closed down with the fall of East Germany and the country's reunification.

Unsurprisingly, Micky's son, Clive, had aviation coursing through his veins. He spotted, modelled, and photographed airliners all the way through his teenage years, although his first period of gainful employment came with a year working for the Sheraton Skyline Hotel. He then started with British Airways, working in Technical Block C, reconciling fares on tickets that had been sold to those travelling on other airlines as well as with BA on their journey.

The correct term is 'prorating' tickets (there is always a technical name for such things). Ever since airlines began to co-operate with each other on certain routes, they have had to pay each other for some journeys. British Airways would sell a ticket for a flight, say from Heathrow to Denver in the USA, as with my flight in June 1986. BA did not fly to Denver at the time, so my flight took me from Heathrow to Chicago, where I cleared immigration and customs before using a United Airlines (UA) flight from O'Hare to Denver. At Chicago I experienced my first customs stop and search; the US officers were polite, friendly, efficient, and were merely doing their job, and one even carried my baggage to the domestic check-in for me and wished me a good flight. The entire journey was on a British Airways-issued ticket, but part of the fare had to be paid to United for the US domestic part of the trip. Rather curiously, I was also stopped and briefly questioned by a customs officer on my return to Heathrow. He was equally polite and equally friendly, and both occasions remain the only time I have ever been stopped to date.

Somebody at British Airways and United would have had to work out how much UA wanted from BA. By the time of my trip, it wasn't Clive Martin; he had moved on to other things with the airline, possibly because he spent as much time staring out the window at aircraft as he did working out his fares and tickets. People work at airports and for airlines mostly because they want to, not because they have to.

The British Airways base at Heathrow occupies a big chunk of the eastern end of Heathrow, at Hatton Cross. Today it doesn't have the same buildings as it did at its height, with some of the original hangars now having been demolished (the hangar used for Concorde being one). There were, however, six technical blocks, A to F, usually referred to as TBA, TBB, TBC and so on. TBA was often called 'The Kremlin' due to its labyrinthine maze of corridors and offices that never saw any sunshine. That's where Clive went to work on keeping track of where the airline's aircraft were while away from Heathrow—particularly those on long-haul journeys, with a Sydney, Australia-bound 747 being away for as much as five days.

With the closure of the West London Air Terminal, Clive moved to Comet House, the airline's headquarters at the time alongside Speedbird House (both hangovers from the BEA and BOAC days). Clive moved into the new world of computers, becoming a shift leader. On the night of 13 July 1995, he discovered a fire; were it not for the quick response of Clive and his colleagues, BA might have come to a full stop with the loss of network connections to the outside world. Clive and his team were given awards by Sir Colin Marshall, British Airways CEO at the time, for their actions.

Clive's final job for BA was working on the inventory of everything put into Terminal 5 when it opened, a task that was not related to the other problems at the terminal's opening. In Clive's case, everything worked just as intended, and he was on the first flight to leave the new terminal (travelling to Paris) on 27 March 2008, retiring after nearly thirty-two years with the airline.

Slightly more than two years after watching the former Concorde hangar disintegrate into a cloud of dust and rubble, Clive's son, Neil, started working at Heathrow in early 1999, aged just fifteen. With his sixteenth birthday coming up in August, Neil could leave school and go and do something worthwhile, like working at LHR:

> I did attempt to stay on at school first, doing three A levels in Physics, Chemistry and Maths—to be a pilot. This dropped quickly to two A levels, Maths and Physics—to be an air traffic controller. But I liked working, making money and the opportunities to travel that it brought, so I left sixth-form college by December.

Aviation is, after all, in the blood. Neil nodded:

> Yes, I did try the academic route, [but] it wasn't for me. I like to learn and [I] love information. However, once I was working and travelling around spotting, I started to lose the dedication needed for A levels.

Travelling as well? I have done more than my share, but Neil probably beats me. He nodded again:

> I travelled alone to various airports. August 1998 was my first trip abroad on my own—to Frankfurt, two days at the airport, spotting. For my birthday, I would ask my dad for various standby tickets around Europe for solo spotting trips.

Terminal 1 (Domestic) in 2002. British Airways introduced a new colour scheme in 1997, with tail fin designs submitted by artists around the world. The idea was not well-received, and by 2002 all were replaced by the Union Flag design. (*Author*)

Terminal 1 in 2002. British Midland Airways had emerged as BA's main competitor both within the UK and in Europe. (*Author*)

As a passenger mobility assistant for a company named Capital Aviation (owned by a father and two sons), Neil's first job was to help those passengers less able to travel the sometimes lengthy distances in the terminal to get to and from their flights:

> You couldn't get a full airport ID until you were sixteen, so I had to be escorted myself using a temporary ID … [this] worked well because on many occasions couples would both need wheelchairs, so I could push one with my escort pushing the other. My birthday was a bit special though.

It was the day of the total solar eclipse, 11 August 1999. The UK doesn't get many, so it's probably a once-in-a-lifetime experience for most people. There was the full deal across Cornwall and the south west of England, but it was only partially visible in London and at Heathrow. It is the only one I have ever seen. I may not have seen the whole thing, but I could still feel a massive chunk of the sun being obscured; it got noticeably darker and colder.

Neil continued:

> Not only was it the day of the eclipse, it was my birthday and the day I could get my full airport ID … it made me the youngest full-ID staff member [at] the airport….
>
> I was waiting in the ID centre in the Queen's Building, watching various training videos and those ahead of me were getting their IDs when we were all reminded that the Eclipse was coming. We rushed out and watched it outside the Queen's Building before returning inside. It was interesting and I'm glad I saw it, but I was really more proud to get the ID.

This was highlight number one then. Neil's brow furrowed as he thought back to the next one:

> I think it was 2000… I had to go and meet a flight at domestic arrivals, pick up this chap, and take him through the arrivals process to the person meeting him, which normally terminates with me taking the passenger to the car outside… I met the gentleman from the flight at Gate 5B. Obviously I had his name, but it didn't mean anything to me at the time. On the way to arrivals we stopped at the gents', and while I was waiting outside, several people, all much older than me—I was only sixteen, remember—asked if they could get his autograph. I said they would have to ask this chap, and I'm thinking, 'Who is this guy?' I didn't know him from anybody else. He eventually returned and people had their autographs and pictures and quick conversations, then we went on our way. He was a nice guy too, very chatty with those who wanted to talk to him, although he did seem a bit eccentric at times, [an] older man obviously, white hair, thick glasses and a rather tatty coat…

No clue as to who he was? Neil shook his head:

> No, not to me anyway. After collecting his bags, I took him to his car and his driver gave me a £5 tip. Tips were gratefully received as a young man, and quite often [they were] enough to cover food and travel costs. I waved at this chap as they drove off, and he gave an enthusiastic wave back … I still didn't know who he was, so I went back to our

office and had to ask, since everybody who worked there was older than me. [I said,] 'Hey everybody, who the heck is Michael Foot?'

Michael Foot was leader of the Labour Party that was soundly defeated by Margaret Thatcher's Conservatives. The Labour Party election manifesto was widely denounced at the time as 'the longest suicide note in history'. While many people disagreed with Foot's policies, he was also equally widely considered to be one of the nicest men in politics. Neil continued:

> When seeing news of his death in March 2010, I thought back to our fifteen minutes together and it still makes me laugh now. He was a genuinely nice guy.

Surely he wasn't the only well-known personality Neil pushed around though? There is something a little appealing about being in complete control of someone famous. I never met Michael Foot, but as one of those who was never in agreement with his politics, the temptation while pushing him down one of Heathrow's many ramps would have been almost overwhelming:

> The actor John Mills was also a regular passenger of mine, and we got on well even to the point you could tell he was glad to see it was me meeting him off the regular Manx Airlines Flight from the Isle of Man … he addressed me by my name … this was great for a young lad to have such a acting legend address me by my name. I met many famous people while working there because we also operated the electrical buggies that quite often featured as getaway vehicles for the rich and famous as they travelled through T1. We would often pick them up from the executive lounge and whisk them to their flight—Eric Sykes, Roger Moore, Sean Connery, Pierce Brosnan, the Beckhams, various singers and pop groups, the list is endless.

One or two of the more well-known personalities have something of a reputation for being less than pleasant on occasion. With both my parents in showbusiness, I spent a fair bit of my time as a teenager in the company of various famous people, but I never met any who were less than forthcoming in the pleasantness stakes. I had to ask Neil if he'd ever experienced any tantrums:

> You get your share of passengers that were annoyed about how their trips was going. However, none really got upset with me—it was normally the airline itself. As for the famous, I found them very pleasant—and grateful that I didn't bombard them with the usual questions and requests for autographs. I made a point never to ask for an autograph because I liked to be that one part of their journey in which they could ride on my electric cart and not get pestered. Everybody's the same when travelling. They just want to get to wherever it is they are going.

I never got anybody's autograph either. Hobnobbing with the rich, powerful, and famous has its attractions, but so does climbing the greasy pole. I asked Neil about his rise to where he is now:

I progressed through to being a Supervisor/Allocator in Capital Aviation, which later got bought out by Groundstar Handling … once I was eighteen, I was able to apply to work at BAA as a security guard. I did this in July 2001 and passed the relevant checks. I was awaiting a start date when the September 11 attacks occurred, which meant the airport didn't know what would happen with passenger numbers and their need for me.

Those old enough to remember US President John F. Kennedy's assassination in Dallas, Texas, often say that they can instantly recall where they were and what they were doing when they heard the news. New York's Idlewild Airport was renamed 'JFK' not long after the shooting. There is probably nobody who was alive on 11 September 2001 that cannot say the same—especially those who earn their living from commercial aviation, like Neil:

I was in Oslo, spotting from the airside area, and saw the news on the [public] TV screens at the airport. I was on standby to return and the flights were getting cancelled, so my chance of getting home was going fast. I was a supervisor by then, and my phone rang … I was needed in work to assist. My office got onto British Airways and my standby ticket was changed from British Airways to Scandinavian Airlines System (SAS), and I was flown back to Heathrow in the jump seat in the cockpit of a SAS MD81. They were using T3 by then, so I went straight from Terminal 3 to Terminal 1 on arrival and spent the time helping passengers get flights and hotels. But it wasn't a nice time for anybody.

In January 2002 I got my start date—1 February 2002 … [it was] only as temporary staff on a six-month contract in Terminal 1, so I took it hoping that I would get a permanent post. This came in June 2002. I was a guard for about a year, and being eighteen, I was probably again one of the youngest working for BAA … I had to prove myself as a decent worker. I quickly progressed to being a stand-in supervisor and then [I] got the security supervisor post full-time in June 2003.

My main job target in BAA was that of Airside Operations, where I would work on the ramps and runways, getting close to the action and [getting to] be around aircraft.

I asked Neil if aircraft were the main point of interest in the Martin family. He nodded:

Oh yeah. I spent just over two years as a supervisor, and on my second attempt I got a job in airside operations in August 2005—still only twenty-two years old—as a movement area assistant. Aircraft marshalling, bird dispersal, and runway inspections form a major part of the job. I then progressed after a time in various stand-up roles, which means filling in temporarily at a job above your normal grade, and [then] secondment officer in airside ops to get the job permanently in June 2011.

I wonder if birds are a particular problem at Heathrow. Most airports have to deal with this, especially those located near the sea. Birds are a big issue at JFK, which lies on the shore of Jamaica Bay in New York. Somewhat strangely, about a quarter of a mile from the end of runway 4 left, which crosses the airport's runway 13 right/31 left at its southern end, there is a bird sanctuary on Joco Marsh—the Jamaica Bay Wildlife Refuge, operated by the New York Harbor Parks Authority. It has been there for decades. On 12 November 1975 (less than five months after JFK's most calamitous disaster, Eastern Flight 66), an Overseas National Airways (ONA) Douglas DC10 started its take-off roll along runway 13 right, the airport's longest at 14,752 feet long. The runway runs alongside Jamaica Bay, hence its colloquial name 'The Bay Runway'. As the DC10 neared its take-off speed, the pilot, Captain Harold Davis, saw a flock of gulls on the aircraft's right side, over the bay. A microsecond later, the number-one engine, on the left side, ingested a bird (or a number of birds), exploded, and fell from its wing mounting and onto the runway, severing the fuel lines and causing a fire. Captain Davis aborted the take-off; with one wing engine now missing, the asymmetric thrust from the other wing engine meant the aircraft left the strip of concrete and finally came to a halt near the far end of the runway, on the grassed area. The flames from the burning wing spread to the rest of the aircraft, which was destroyed.

As luck would have it, the flight was a company charter, and all those on board worked for ONA. They were therefore fully trained in emergency procedures, so everybody escaped unharmed, although the runway was littered with the remains of a number of seagulls. In the days of propeller aircraft, the spinning prop presented more of a hazard to the average bird, but now it's the other way around; a jet engine is like a giant vacuum cleaner, and it doesn't respond well to sucking in anything but air (although it does cope well with water and rain).

There are no bird sanctuaries around Heathrow, but Neil remains justifiably proud of the airport's good record:

> I don't think our level is any higher than expected. However, we are always looking to reduce the possibility of birdstrikes and we use all the regular bird-scaring techniques, as at other airports. We do not use dogs or birds of prey, but we do have Tarsier.

A tarsier is a nocturnal arboreal prosimian primate found in the Phillipines and Indonesia; in other words, it is close to a lemur. However, the Tarsier Neil is referring to is a high-resolution ground-observing radar that constantly sweeps the runway for potentially hazardous objects—including birds. Heathrow's Tarsier system was developed by QinetiQ and has been in use since 2008. The company issued a press release announcing the system:

> As the world's busiest international airport, handling over 60m passengers each year, the safety responsibilities of Heathrow's Airside Safety Department (ASD) are immense. The safe passage of every one of those travellers is paramount in everything the airport does, and with growth beginning to return to the industry, the size of this task is set to increase. The safety record at Heathrow is one of which we are proud, and we continuously look to set the standard across the industry. For any airport operator, the area of highest risk is the runway. Risks can range from a disabled aircraft stranded on the runway, through a roosting flock of birds to a single item of debris, such as the metallic strip which led to

A Hitchcockian fantasy outside Hatton Cross Station, right next to the final approach path of runway 27 left. (*Author*)

Fantasy or nightmare? (*Author*)

the Concorde tragedy in Paris ten years ago. At Heathrow, runways are inspected visually to twice the internationally recommended standard, however the incident at Charles de Gaulle showed that even the biggest airports with the most rigorous procedures can carry a residual risk. And short of inspecting the runway after every arrival or departure, visual inspections can only go so far in reducing this risk.

Heathrow is still one of the world's safest airports, and Neil is just one of many who continue to help it stay that way:

I recently [reached] ten years in airfield ops in August 2015, and I can't think of any job better than that on the airfield. It truly is, as so many people say, a 'dead man's shoes' job... The only time a vacancy comes up is if someone dies or retires.

This won't be any time soon for Neil—the Martin flag will continue to fly over Heathrow for some while yet.

In 2005, a van marked 'Follow Me' guides an Aeroflot Ilyushin IL76 freighter to the cargo area. (*Simon Boddy*)

Most passenger aircraft stands have an automatic lighting system that tells the aircraft which way to go and when to stop. At the cargo centre, an aircraft marshaller does the job the traditional way. (*Simon Boddy*)

Above: The IL76 was carrying vehicles and equipment for the visit of President Vladimir Putin. (*Simon Boddy*)

Below: Right a bit... (*Simon Boddy*)

Right a bit more... (*Simon Boddy*)

Go straight... and stop. (*Simon Boddy*)

12
Sniffing the Atmosphere

I think it is a pity to lose the romantic side of flying and simply to accept it as a common means of transport.

Amy Johnson

In the USA, they used to call them 'fence-sitters'—young kids who would ride their bikes out to their local airport and lean on the fence by the terminal, watching as shiny airliners—the old ones with whirly things on the front of the engines—came and went. They were dreaming of the day when they would leave the confines of childhood behind, joining the smartly dressed grown-ups walking out to their futuristic, gleaming machines before soaring aloft, riding the clouds to some exotic, far-away city hitherto found only in their fertile and enquiring young minds.

In the UK and Europe, it wasn't quite the same—most airports didn't have a fence to sit on. Still, they did have areas set aside to watch the comings and goings of aircraft; these spaces often had tables and chairs, and sometimes even a play area for those still too young to really appreciate the majesty of the technological advances unfolding just a few yards away. The fence-sitters still existed just the same, and just like their aviation-minded cousins across the Atlantic, the same dreams filled their youthful imaginations.

The airports, along with the young, grew rapidly—very rapidly, to the point where the fence no longer existed as the space was taken up by expanded terminals. Not that this stopped the fence-sitter, who morphed into the modern-day equivalent and spent his (or sometimes her) time at the heady heights of the new buildings, still having the same dreams and still watching the arrivals and departures from the airport observation deck. In the case of Heathrow, it was the roof gardens of the Queens Building and the Europa Building.

Future pilots, cabin crew, engineers, air traffic controllers, and even those oft-hard-pressed airline check-in agents, along with those who simply liked airlines and airports, spent days and sometimes nights atop the airport's terminal. Hopeful aviation photographers and writers began to learn their craft there—not just at Heathrow, but everywhere else as well, at least as long as they had enough money to buy film and pay for it to be developed and printed. When they didn't, they just watched. The observation deck was also a place for all those friends and relatives as their loved ones departed and arrived. As a bonus, they provided some useful revenue for the airport.

Growing up brings new challenges and changes. Some of the fence-sitters went on to fulfil their dreams. Some found that life got in the way and went on to do other things—sometimes more mundane, and sometimes just as vibrant and exciting as flying for a living. Just as life changes, so did the observation deck. New concerns and new fears—some real, some imagined—meant the disappearance of those much-cherished places where anybody could meet and greet, or take photographs, or just watch, sinking blissfully into their surroundings. New terminals replaced what often became cramped and crowded buildings that nevertheless had served the thousands who travelled by air well (and occasionally not so well). However, most of the newest terminals, including those at Heathrow, do not include anywhere to observe; for those who just want to watch or take pictures, the observation deck became an endangered species.

Heathrow's recently built passenger facilities—from Terminal 4, which opened in 1986, to Terminal 5 and Terminal 2 The Queen's Terminal—has seen the demolition of the airport's original buildings. The iconic control tower is gone, as is the Queen's Building, and, alongside it, what became the (old) Terminal 2, with its famous rooftop viewing area.

To watch and photograph airliners arriving at Heathrow today means taking the tube to Hatton Cross (if arrivals are using runway 27 left) and crossing the Great South West Road, turning right and walking under the steel frames of the approach lights to a small park almost opposite the threshold of the runway. It is known as 'Myrtle Avenue' after the side road that leads to it. On a sunny morning, landing aircraft seem almost close enough to touch as they swoop over the busy main road, past the park, and down to the runway. Even the most modest camera can catch good shots, and some of the photographs in this book were taken from there. There are other locations around Heathrow's perimeter; if landings are from the east, they are always to runway 09 left; the Thistle Hotel, on the Bath Road, almost opposite Terminal 5, has a good bar open to non-residents. However, none of this is the same as a well-placed on-airport observation deck.

Gatwick's panoramic views are also gone, seemingly for good. New York's JFK has new terminals around its central area, and the equally famous car park on top of the former Pan Am terminal disappeared with its demolition. In both cases, no observation decks will be available to the twenty-first-century fence-sitter (unless you're a passenger—Heathrow's Terminal 4 does have one airside for those travelling somewhere). It's not all bad news, however. At the time of writing, Manchester still remains the best venue in the UK for watching heavy metal. Most German airports still have officially approved areas to watch aircraft; although the ability to get up close and personal to Lufthansa's fleet at Frankfurt has gone, there is a good view from Terminal 2's open-air deck. Amsterdam and Zurich remain two of the must-visit airports for the fence-sitter. Paris Charles de Gaulle has restrictions, but Orly's deck is still there. Further afield, one can get good views at both Tokyo Haneda and Narita, as well as at Nagoya and Osaka. Singapore, Seoul, Sydney, and Perth all have places to watch and photograph what comes and goes. At Hong Kong, the famous checkerboard approach may be a memory, but Chep Lap Kok's Sky Deck permits excellent views of the tarmac, and it is also part of the larger aviation discovery centre, complete with museum and interactive exhibits.

While some of the closures came as a result of terminal expansion and what is sometimes referred to as 'repurposing' areas once given over to viewing, many of the

Hatton Cross underground station. Alight here, check out the BOAC speedbird logos, and head for Myrtle Avenue. (*Author*)

Hatton Cross Station. To the left is the BA maintenance base and to the right is the Great Southwest Road. (*Author*)

A little imagination can produce some interesting views from the station precincts. (*Author*)

Another view from the station. (*Author*)

Giants at rest—the BA maintenance base. (*Leo Martin*)

Hatton Cross. At one time, the road in the centre led through the middle of the base and a set of traffic lights were used to halt vehicles if the taxiway was in use. (*Author*)

Looking south, away from London, along the Great Southwest Road. Allegedly, it was once the haunt of Dick Turpin. (*Author*)

The last house before touchdown. (*Author*)

Above left: Dull days, approach lights, and large Malaysians. (*Author*)

Above right: The famous statue, now not far from its original location on the northern perimeter road. (*Author*)

Below: Spotter's paradise; the only official viewing platform at Heathrow. There is a high fence between it and the northern runway. (*Author*)

The message is loud and clear, although in July 2015 it didn't stop protesters from cutting through this very fence for the sit-in on the piano keys of runway 27 right. (*Author*)

After breakfast and ready for some photography. (*Author*)

restrictions understandably arose as a result of acts of terrorism against the USA and its airlines—9/11 especially. It's therefore all the more remarkable that there are, in fact, numerous observation areas available at many US airports. Baltimore, Dallas/ Fort Worth, Grand Rapids, and Minneapolis/St. Paul, amongst others, all have areas available for spotting, photography, or just looking. Even the famous Theme Building has reopened its deck beneath the parabolic arches at Los Angeles.

All this does rather beg the question: why can't it be done at New York—or London? An obvious answer is that all three New York airports—JFK, La Guardia, and Newark— and Heathrow and Gatwick are prime targets for those with sinister aims. Yet what is preferable? To have those genuinely interested in aviation at safe, secure, and supervised locations, or to have them skulking around the airport's perimeters?

At Heathrow, there is at least one official way of skulking; an application to the Metropolitan Police for an enthusiast's identity card gives the holder official recognition that he or she is an enthusiast and has a legitimate reason for being around the airport's outer borders. The card is also eligible for use at London City Airport.

This, of course, brings new meaning to the term fence-sitting. It is something, at least, and all the more worthy for its existence, but it's not the same as being able to immerse yourself on an open-air observation deck on a terminal roof, where the sights, sounds and aromas of commercial aviation can waft over one's senses - where you can sniff the atmosphere.

As yet, there is no similar ID scheme on the other side of the Atlantic, at JFK, and the airport is all the poorer for it. The redevelopment of all the central area terminals was in many ways a missed opportunity—with the exception of the former Braniff building, now the only terminal still in its original form and used by Delta for the carrier's domestic operations. If the airport had incorporated secure locations for photographers, spotters, and the friends and relatives of those actually going somewhere, they could have propelled the airport into the same bracket as Amsterdam and Zurich. The same could and perhaps should be applied to London's airports.

The pictorial records that remain of the past are quite valuable—those surviving first pictures, some of which are good, and some not so good. The grainy images produced are the result of the average pre-teen and teenage aviation enthusiast's early efforts to record what came and went—the memories of a childhood spent on airport observation decks. Printed photographs that have been stashed away for years take on a new meaning; they are a reminder of days gone by, of aircraft and airlines no longer gracing the ramp, paid for first with pocket money and later a spare few pounds or dollars from what remains after paying the bills.

Paradoxically, it has never been easier for people to take photographs. The arrival of the digital era has meant the economics of photography has changed completely. The opportunity to take hundreds of pictures now exists where it didn't before. Concerns over how many individual images would be out of focus, too blurred, or just not quite what one intended are no longer a worry, and neither are the costs that go along with it. Discarding the not so good and keeping the best has become an easy and inexpensive process, which has the added benefit of improving the learning curve for the aspiring photographer, both young and not so young. Still, for all that, the fence sitter still needs a fence to sit on.

To most people, the average enthusiast, whatever they enthuse about, is male, either middle-aged or retired, has a beard, and wears an anorak. Personally, I haven't seen

The northern perimeter road, which runs along the path of the original taxiway that served Heathrow's first runway. (*Author*)

Crouch down, poke the lens through the fence... The remains of the taxiway can be seen in the foreground. (*Author*)

Comings and goings. Runway 27 right's threshold, with the BA base behind. (*Author*)

BA's Airbus A380. (*Author*)

Four for the price of one—five if one counts the green mock-up on the right, which is used to train the emergency services to rescue people from crashed and burning aircraft. (*Author*)

Head-on; one of British Airways' increasingly large fleet of Airbus A380s turns onto runway 27 right for take-off. (*Author*)

A meeting of minds as a 777 departs, and a 747 holds. (*Author*)

Taking photographs into the sun from anywhere on the north side of the airport can cause problems, but it can also produce some good results. (*Author*)

anybody fitting such a description, whether they are parked at the end of a railway station platform, a bus station, or an airport—although I'm sure there are some.

Tyler McDowell and Leo Martin (no relation to Micky, Clive, or Neil) are as far away from the perception as you can get. Both are still in their teens—Tyler is nineteen and Leo is eighteen—but their passion is as great as any of the fence-sitters of days gone by. Tyler was three years old the first time he went to Heathrow, his first flight being on British Airways Boeing 777 G-VIIM in 2000. Leo was six when he took his first flight from Heathrow, a BA flight to Toronto.

I don't know where my interest in commercial aviation came from, and I was never brainy enough to be a pilot; at least Tyler and Leo live close by and have grown up with the airport. Both aim to work in aviation. Tyler told me he didn't have a particular aim in mind, but any role within the airport or one of the airlines would do. Leo was a little more definitive:

> Since I was very young I've wanted to work in one area or another. I went to a flight training exhibition, which showed how I could become a pilot, but the cost rather put me off, so I've looked at the apprenticeships offered by both Heathrow and British Airways. I'll be applying in 2016.

Maybe the cost is one reason why I never looked into being a pilot. I could handle the stick and rudder part of flying an aircraft, but the mental acrobatics is another matter, even if I did have lots of money. In the meantime, both teenagers can be found, cameras in hand, photographing arrivals and departures somewhere around the perimeter. Leo continued:

> The airport police don't seem to mind spotters taking photographs these days, plus I've found people can be very kind. Although the airport doesn't serve spotters as such, they don't ban or penalize [them] and [they] allow people to go where they like—within reason.

Tyler commented on the viewing facilities at the airport:

> I don't like how they did away with the viewing deck on the old Terminal 2 and haven't put in another one. They have got one in Terminal 4 but it's airside, so only passengers flying from the terminal can use it. I still love Heathrow and its variety of airlines, and there are plenty of places to watch them from. While they're not official or as good as the old deck on T2, you do get interesting movements.

Fay Jordan is another who doesn't fit the average description of an aircraft enthusiast. As her name implies, she isn't male, and she happily describes herself as an 'avgeek', visiting Heathrow regularly to photograph aircraft:

> It's a downside that photographers don't seem to be as welcome at Heathrow as much as they are at Manchester, Amsterdam, or Frankfurt. The atmosphere [from officialdom] isn't in any way intimidating and you are left alone unless you're doing something stupid, but we aren't made to feel welcome at all. There are no official spotting areas apart from a useless (from a photography standpoint) bus-shelter-type thing on the other side of the northern perimeter

road since the Queen's Building closed. While the powers-that-be aren't particularly hostile towards enthusiasts, I think they would prefer it if we weren't there at all.

Many others agree with Fay's comments, including Steve Hopwood. Born and bred in Manchester, Steve has lived in the north-western city all his life. He inherited his interest from his father, who served in the RAF before going to work for Avro, Hawker Siddeley, and BAe.

The A. V. Roe Aeroplane Company built the Second World War Lancaster bomber (among other types), from which the Lancastrian airliner was developed—the same Lancastrian that flew the first service from Heathrow. Hawker Siddeley came up with the Trident (originally developed by de Havilland), with which Heathrow was synonymous throughout the 1960s and 1970s. The British Aircraft Corporation, now known as BAe, built the BAC111. Steve related:

> My first visit to Heathrow was in 1970, which was a real eye-opener to a young lad whose only other airport visit was Ringway [Manchester], which wasn't exactly buzzing back then. At Heathrow, [there was] the international flavour, with airlines flying in from all over the world, the constant activity, and the fact that the central area, being isolated from the rest of reality, was like a small town devoted to commercial aviation—the magic of approaching the tunnel adorned with that big sign, 'Welcome To Heathrow'. Only Salzburg and Las Vegas have the same first impressions....
>
> They have the 'wow' factor. Going into the tunnel at Heathrow, beneath that sign, is a bit special, and so are both of the [other] cities. Vegas you can understand, but Salzburg is a bit special as well.

I have been to neither of those cities yet, but I have used the Heathrow tunnel more than a few times. Steve's memories of pre-redevelopment times are pretty clear. He can remember comparing Heathrow and his hometown airport:

> [In the] early days they both had excellent viewing facilities, but Heathrow won hands down on activity and variety. As the years went by, both lost the classic spectator terraces.

Heathrow held on to the roof gardens, albeit in a much-reduced size, until 2002. Manchester's went in the late 1990s; in both cases, spectators found refuge on multi-storey car parks. Steve continued:

> Present-day Manchester wins with the Aviation Viewing Park, but I've no idea how long [the] enlargement of Terminal 2 at MAN will [take]. And, like Heathrow, it looks like the original terminal will be lost as well.

Manchester's viewing park sits to the south of the present terminal complex, alongside the runway and taxiway. It comes complete with a Concorde and the last Trident 3, which sat at LHR for years, used as a training aid, after being withdrawn from service. It was moved to Manchester after being threatened with scrapping. Despite his long-standing interest in civil aviation (he's also a very good model builder), Steve is not a regular visitor these days:

March 2003 was the last time. Ironically, it was the only time I used Heathrow with both my mum and dad … [We and] a group of family friends … attended a friend's memorial service in Southampton. I would like to use Heathrow more, but these days Manchester has grown so much there isn't the need there once was. I can only envisage an enthusiast's trip in future, and then only if it was worth it from the viewing standpoint.

Above: Although the fence is an issue, Heathrow's northern perimeter would offer a number of suitable places for an official (and supervised) observation point—if the airport was willing to do something about it. (*Author*)

Below: The new Terminal 2, just out of sight to the right, is the home of the Star Alliance group of airlines, including United Airlines and (as seen in the background) TAP Air Portugal and Singapore Airlines. (*Author*)

Myrtle Avenue Park, right on the Great Southwest Road, a few minutes' walk south from Hatton Cross Station, and just over the road from the threshold of runway 27 left. (*Leo Martin*)

Enthusiasts. (*Author*)

More enthusiasts. (*Author*)

The A380 is a head-turner even when landing on the far side of the airport, on 27 right. (*Author*)

The nesting place for spotters and photographers is under the trees, behind the bushes, and out of sight. An Asiana Boeing 777 touches down on 27 left, as seen from Myrtle Avenue Park. (*Author*)

Over the rooftops. Often used in sensationalist media, the houses on Myrtle Avenue itself are actually set well back from the approach path to 27 left, but a different impression can be given depending on where one stands when taking a photograph. (*Author*)

Stormy days. (*Author*)

Rainbow days. (*Author*)

Sunny days and a little creativity under the approach lights. (*Author*)

Myrtle Avenue allows the photographer to get up close and personal to this Qantas Airbus A380. (*Author*)

An Emirates Airlines A380. (*Author*)

Over the Great Southwest Road, over the fence, and across the threshold of 27 left. (*Author*)

The Airbus A380 is unquestionably big. (*Author*)

13

Protest

We want the air to unite the peoples and not to divide them.

Lord Swinton

On 26 February 1993, a 2,000-lb bomb exploded in the basement area of the World Trade Center in New York. The bomber's intention had been to topple one of the twin towers into the other. Damage to the underground floors was extensive, but if the explosion was a wake-up call, nobody got up.

In *The Airport: Terminal Nights and Runway Days at John F. Kennedy International* (1994), author James Kaplan interviewed Captain Frank Fox, then with JFK's special-planning office. Fox stated:

> It's just impractical for Mid-East organisations to import terrorism here. It's too far away. It's easier for them to get attention closer to home, for a lot less money. It's all economics … the threat of terrorism in this country is very low. Would the IRA put a bomb on a British Airways plane taking off from Kennedy? It is unlikely. Why? It's a question of money. The IRA is smart. They know that if the battlefield came here, their contributions from the States would dry up.

It is often unacknowledged that despite the United States' relationship with the UK, large amounts of funding went from the US to the IRA—particularly from Boston and the north east, where a significantly large part of the population has Irish ancestry. It is therefore overwhelmingly ironic that Boston was the starting point for the most cataclysmic event in commercial aviation history.

Some years before the bomb went off in New York in February 1993, the IRA had already set up a mortar outside Heathrow's perimeter. They used it to fire shells into the airport, although they landed on the grass areas between the runways and caused no damage. The Army patrolled the terminals at the time and have done so on a number of occasions since. From 1984, it has been routine to see armed police officers strolling through the crowds, their presence reassuring and yet also a reminder that things are not what they used to be. Nevertheless, security has been an issue for some time; on 17 April 1986, just two weeks after my return from New York on Pan Am's *Clipper Neptune's Car*, an attempt to place a bomb on board an El Al flight to Tel Aviv was foiled. Bombs had exploded at Heathrow before that—most notably in Terminal 1 in May 1974. T2 also saw one in April 1984.

In December 1988, just three weeks before *Clipper Maid of the Seas* was brought down, I was questioned about my bags as I checked in for my second trip to JFK on Pan Am. Lockerbie was just over four years before the World Trade Center's basement bombing in 1993. Almost nine years later, on 11 September 2001, the airline industry and airports changed forever.

I don't need to recount the details here; it's been done too many times already. Nevertheless, the effect on all the airlines, all airports, and everyone who uses them is still irrevocably felt today. By 2001, Pan Am, the biggest corporate victim of Lockerbie, had been gone for three months short of a decade. What had been done in the almost thirteen years between December 1988 and September 2001?

Airport observation decks were closed, even though airliner enthusiasts and photographers are the least likely group to pose any threat. Bags were searched (again) and x-rayed some more, and yet more questions were asked. However, if somebody is determined enough and patient enough, they will find a way to achieve their aims.

When the UK Airport Runway Commission enquiry into where a new runway should be sited came out in favour of a third runway at Heathrow, there were predictable and immediate howls of outrage from various pressure groups, including, and most understandably, from those who will lose their homes if the runway is built.

The commission's recommendation was just that—a recommendation. According to the government, the final decision was to be made by the end of 2015. The runway will not be built and opened for use for another fifteen years, which makes protests now seem a little premature. Premature or not, at 3.30 a.m. on 13 July, a group of protesters cut through the chain-link fence on the northern perimeter road and staged a sit-in on the threshold of runway 27 right. They were from a group named 'Plane Stupid', which is concerned about the environmental impact of a third runway at LHR. Rather conveniently, the group (along with almost everybody else) either doesn't know or ignores the fact that Heathrow actually had three operational runways until work began on the new Terminal 2. Their sit-in had little effect; arrivals on the southern runway, 27 left, continued uninterrupted, and departures were able to start their take-off run further along the runway, which is, after all, 3,902 metres long. The most the group got was a small amount of publicity, but there was not much of it and most of it was deservedly critical.

Heathrow has seen numerous protests and mass gatherings, from hordes of screaming teenagers yelling at The Beatles to then-student-leader Tariq Ali's demonstrations—both in the '60s. Generally speaking, however, demonstrations have not caused too much of a problem. One rather spectacular failure was organised by a group calling themselves 'CHAOS', which stood for 'Close Heathrow Airport On Sundays'. In early 1970, the group attempted to blockade the airport by gathering thousands on foot, on bicycles, and in cars, circling the roundabout at the entrance to the tunnel on the Bath Road. Only a few cars turned up. There are those who do, and there are those who don't; the difference between angry letter-writers featured in newspapers (of which there are many) and those who will actually do something, however misguided, can be markedly noticeable.

The Metropolitan Police have had responsibility for Heathrow since 1974, and it's a testimony to their work that Heathrow has by and large remained a secure airport in terms of passenger safety. The Met, as they are most often known, also have in place the earlier-mentioned identity scheme for enthusiasts and photographers. Upon successful application, the enthusiast will receive an identity card enabling them to spend time at the airport perimeter with their cameras and notebooks. The card is also valid at London City Airport, but not, curiously, at Gatwick or Stansted. The biggest advantage to the scheme is that the enthusiasts also provide additional ears and eyes for the police—a mirror of an identical scheme at Minneapolis/Saint Paul Airport (MSP) in the United States. Applicants for the ID card at MSP are vetted and actually given some basic training in assisting with watching for any unusual activity.

The biggest cause for concern over people in and around the airport usually arises when delays to aircraft movements (inbound or outbound) mean the terminals and the surrounding roads get congested. Delays can happen due to weather, air traffic control problems, or strikes. Today, strikes are not often the cause of delays in the UK, although Heathrow does have its occasional moments. The French, however, are famous for it, even in the twenty-first century. Those living in the County of Kent, on the other side of London from Heathrow, regularly see their roads clogged by traffic, most of it heavy-goods vehicles. The port of Dover and its cross-channel ferries grind to a complete halt, held up by strikes at Calais, on the other side of the Channel. If French air traffic controllers go on strike—as they often do during the height of summer—flights travelling through French airspace will be delayed.

Strikes are not confined to Heathrow or France. Germany's Hamburg Airport temporarily shut its terminal building in February 2015 after a strike by security staff caused overcrowding. The delays caused five-hour waits in security queues, with the police closing the doors to the terminal building two hours after the strike began. The twenty-four-hour strike was called by the trade union, Verdi, which was trying to ensure higher wages for its members.

Whatever the cause of a strike, the knock-on effect can be devastating to passengers and airlines. Aircraft have to wait longer to take off and land, meaning fuel is wasted. Leaving inbound aircraft in the holding stack has a damaging effect on both the economy and the environment; the needless burning of fuel releases unnecessarily large amounts of CO_2 into the atmosphere.

14
Control and Regulation

The most beautiful dream that has haunted the heart of man since Icarus is today reality.

Louis Bleriot

In 1986, the BBC ran a series of daily television programmes from Heathrow. Broadcast on BBC One during the early afternoon, each programme looked at various aspects of life at the airport, and one included an interview with an air traffic controller. He was asked how aircraft were guided along the runways and in the skies above the UK, and he described how operations were controlled down to a particular height. When the interviewer asked what happened below that particular height, the air traffic controller replied, 'Below that, it's very much a see-and-be-seen form of control.'

The remark caused something of a storm, with a flood of calls to the BBC and the Civil Aviation Authority from concerned viewers. They had nightmare visions of pilots myopically peering out of their cockpit windows, unable to see another fast-moving airliner (especially in cloud), meaning that only luck would prevent a mid-air collision. These mid-air collisions have happened, but not in the UK.

In 1960, a United Airlines Douglas DC8 *en route* from Chicago to Idlewild and a TWA Lockheed Constellation *en route* to La Guardia from Columbus, Ohio, collided over New York, crashing into Brooklyn. All 164 souls on board the two aircraft died, along with six on the ground. It was a collision between the new—the DC8—and the old—the Constellation.

On the morning of 10 September 1976, an Inex-Adria Airlines Douglas DC9 departed from Split, in what was then Yugoslavia, for Cologne, Germany. At Heathrow, BEA flight BE476, operated by Trident 3B G-AWZT, took off for Istanbul. British Airways had been founded by then, but the full integration of BEA and BOAC was still underway, so the BEA flight still used its existing call sign and flight number prefix. At 10.14 a.m., the two aircraft collided; the two major sections of what remained of the planes came to rest 4 miles apart, some 16 miles from Zagreb. One hundred and seventy-six people lost their lives.

Sunday 27 March 1977 remains one of commercial aviation's blackest days. At a fogbound Tenerife, KLM Royal Dutch Airlines Boeing 747 PH-BUF collided with Pan Am Boeing 747 N736PA, causing the deaths of 583 people. As if to mock the many people with a fear of flying, the collision happened on the ground—just as with the 737 engine fire at Manchester in 1985, eight years later. The KLM aircraft was on its take-off run and the Pan Am 747 was still on the runway ahead of it. The accident remains the worst in the history of civil aviation.

If it had existed in 1977, Tarsier ground radar could have helped to prevent the collision. The quest to make flying safer is never-ending; all three of the accidents mentioned above directly led to worldwide improvements in air traffic control and radar—like Tarsier. At the time of writing, there has never been a mid-air collision in UK airspace; there have been near misses, although most are considerably exaggerated by some news outlets. Airline disasters make good headlines, but UK air traffic controllers are still the best in the world.

The BBC-interviewed controller reappeared on a subsequent broadcast and clarified what he had meant. He was, in fact, referring to what happens when aircraft are below the height at which they are given their usual in-flight instructions. At this stage, they come under the direction of airport control towers. Pilots will be looking out of the cockpit window and observing the runways of the airport ahead, but they will still be under the guidance and control of the airport tower, whose radar will identify each and every aircraft. Every airport tower must have clear and unobstructed views of every part of the airport they control—the reasons for this are obvious.

Heathrow's old control tower did not have these views, although it did when it was first built and opened alongside the Europa Building and the Queen's Building in 1955. It was situated in the very centre of the Heathrow, representing the airport's heart. By the time it closed, however, the continually expanding terminals had begun to block views of major parts of the taxiways (although not the runways). In addition to this, with the airport's development gradually shifting the facilities further east and Terminal 5 about to be built, the control tower was not in the centre any more. Terminal 5 would also be built high enough to block the tower's views of the ends of runway 9 left and right. Before work began on the new terminal, a taller tower needed to be built.

The new control tower cost £50 million and was positioned just off the northern end of the cross pier of Terminal 3. It is a free-standing structure and looks a little like an afterthought; in some ways, this is true, as it wasn't part of T3's original design. It now sits neatly in what has become Heathrow's most central location. The new tower is one of the tallest in Europe and came into use in April 2007.

In the UK, air traffic control falls under the jurisdiction of the UK's National Air Traffic Services. Usually referred to simply as 'NATS', the organisation is the main air-navigation service provider across the country. It was originally formed in 1962, inheriting the traditions of UK Air Traffic Control, which was founded at Croydon Airport and was the world's first air traffic control service. Today, NATS controls all air movements over UK airspace (including Royal Air Force and other military operations in conjunction with the RAF's own air traffic control services) and also provides ATC services at fourteen of the UK's airports, including Heathrow. As well as controlling and guiding commercial air traffic along the UK's air corridors, NATS also covers aircraft over much of the North Atlantic—aircraft either bound for or leaving from UK airports or merely flying over the UK to Europe and elsewhere.

All of this might sound a little confusing, but the system works well. NATS's business is regulated and operated under licence from the Civil Aviation Authority, otherwise known as the CAA. The CAA is a public corporation that was established by parliament in 1972 as the UK's national aviation regulator. It was also the provider of air traffic control services at the time. NATS was separated from the CAA in the late 1990s, becoming a public and private partnership organisation in 2001.

Put simply, the CAA is British aviation's governing body. It addresses every sector of aviation in the country, from safety and airspace management to economics and consumer protection, from the Airbus A380 to private aircraft and air displays. If an individual wants to run an airport, the CAA must check them over and give them a licence; even Heathrow is licensed by the CAA. The organisation offers guidelines on its website:

Guidance for airline operators and staff:

Flights carrying fare-paying passengers, or cargo for which payment has been taken, must be operated by companies or individuals holding specific safety approvals and commercial licences which ensure the passenger is appropriately protected.

Companies or individuals must hold an Air Operator's Certificate (AOC) which is granted by the CAA to companies or individuals that have shown they meet the higher safety standards required to carry fare-paying passengers. This covers the entire operation from the training and experience of the crew to the maintenance of the aircraft and planning of the flights.

Most air operators will also need to hold an Operating Licence, in line with European Council requirements governing the operation of air services within the European Economic Area (EEA). In order to be granted an Operating Licence, air operators must satisfy the CAA that, amongst other aspects, they hold appropriate passenger and third party insurance and that they are majority owned and controlled by EEA nationals. Airlines operating aircraft with 20 seats or more must also satisfy the CAA that they have in place sufficient funding to support the business.

The CAA has continuous oversight of AOC and Operating Licence holders and can remove the certificate or licence at any time if it feels that the company cannot maintain the required safety standards or no longer meets the necessary criteria for holding an Operating Licence.

The CAA regulates:

Active professional and private pilots (50,000)
Licensed aircraft engineers (12,400)
Air traffic controllers (2,350)
Commercial Air Operators, including airlines (206)
Licensed aerodromes (141)
Organisations involved in the design, production and maintenance of aircraft (950)
Aircraft registered in the UK (19,000)
ATOL holders (2,400)

ATOL stands for 'Air Travel Organiser's Licence' and is the means whereby holidaymakers are offered protection in case of the travel firm they booked with going out of business. This has happened, most notably with the collapse of Court Line Aviation on 15 August

1974. Thousands were stranded at holiday hotspots, unable to get home. Court Line's problems were due to its business being derived almost exclusively from Clarkson's Tours; when that company went bankrupt, it took the airline with it.

However, the CAA do not currently regulate drones, although there are some limited powers over their use. Drones are several steps up from the radio-controlled model aircraft that have been around for years, and the British have taken to them with gusto. Over the course of 2015, sales have quadrupled. There is some regulation in place for model aircraft, although it must be said that almost all model-aircraft owners operate them with discretion and common sense.

There are, of course, exceptions. Over the Christmas and New Year period of 2008, a person or persons unknown unsuccessfully attempted to fly a model radio-controlled helicopter over the prison wall at HMP Elmley, on the Isle of Sheppey, Kent. The helicopter was carrying a cargo of drugs intended for one of the prison's residents. According to the UK Ministry of Justice, there were seven drone seizures between February and May 2015—two examples being a drone found stuck in the razor wire at Bedford Prison and another crashing on its way into Whatton Prison. One has to wonder how many successful flights have been made into prisons.

Outside military use, the consistent rise of the drone has been fuelled by keen amateurs wanting to film their house, birthday party, and so on. They have also been used by equally amateur photography fans wanting to get a unique set of air-to-ground images. This is fine up to a point, but no background checks are made and no operating license is required to fly drones. Anybody can buy one of these comparatively unobtrusive aerial machines and voyeuristically film people, stealthily trespass, and crash spectacularly. Drones also have the potential to cause a crash; they are generally not very large, but a collision between a drone and commercial airliner could be catastrophic, and there has already been one recorded instance of a drone being used near Heathrow. Drones could also be used in acts of terrorism. Early in 2015, Lord West, a former aviation security minister, proposed a number of measures to tackle this problem, but they were deflected by the government, who said it was 'closely monitoring the situation'—political speak for 'not doing very much'.

At least the CAA has attempted to do something, which is better than doing nothing. They have introduced a 'drone code', prohibiting drone flying 'beyond the operator's sight' or 500 meters horizontally and 120 meters vertically. It also instructs drone operators to avoid aircraft, airports, and airfields. Drones fitted with cameras must not be flown within 50 meters of buildings or people, nor must they be flown over congested areas such as music concerts. The CAA has not explained how it intends to enforce this code.

Richard Briggs worked for the CAA, and his job meant he spent a considerable time on the runways and in the control tower at Heathrow:

I started in the Control Tower for the CAA in September 1972 as a radio technician. I completed a three-year apprenticeship at Bletchley Park (Civil Aviation Signals and Training Establishment—CASTE). The apprenticeship was excellent and is a model of what should be done for 'non-university types' these days. As a young man interested in aviation, being surrounded by aircraft on a day-to-day basis as well as the general buzz of life [was exciting].

At Heathrow, I did routine maintenance and fault-fixing of the air traffic communications systems, including remote transmitter and receiver sites.

One of those sites was by the sewage works at Perry Oaks and the other at Faggs Road, near the Green Man pub.

I didn't stay at Heathrow for my whole time with the CAA; I worked in other locations over the years before leaving and joining an external IT company ... Shift working was not to my liking, although the 20 per cent uplift on pay was...

One of the drawbacks to working in commercial aviation is shift work. Getting out of bed at 3 a.m. to start work at 5 or 6 a.m. can be a little off-putting. Pilots and cabin crew are known to opt for routes that mean spending less time away from home and more sociable hours as they progress upwards through seniority lists; the newest recruits always get the most awkward schedules. It was ever-thus, and it is mirrored in almost all walks of life.

Still, there were always moments to make up for the awkward hours:

Probably the most funny was when I visited Heathrow in another role before actually working there permanently. In 1972 I was attached to the CAA's Civil Aviation Flying Unit—or CAFU—based at Stansted. One of the purposes of CAFU was to test the Instrument Landing Systems (ILS) at airports around the UK.

Testing the ILS at an airport was achieved by setting up a measuring instrument called a telecrosope at the edge of the runway ... attached to cables that fed equipment in a specially equipped car parked 100 meters or so away (typically on the grass by the runway). The telecroscope resembled a large film camera. Obviously, air traffic control at the airport would be told that there would be this equipment and a car at the edge of the runway between certain times. An aircraft from CAFU would then fly numerous approaches (using ILS) and, on each approach, a bright lamp on the front would be used track the aircraft and record its exact approach. Using the information gained from our equipment (and equipment on the aircraft) it could be determined whether the ILS at the airport was calibrated correctly.

One day I was lucky enough go to Heathrow Airport. We set up at the edge of 27 right, which was being used for landings that day. The weather was gorgeous and a lot of time was spent waiting between approaches performed by our aircraft. During that time I sat and watched all the airliners line up and take off. I took some great photographs.

We'd been there for about four hours when we saw a black and yellow CAA Land Rover come hurtling down the runway towards us. It screeched to a halt and some red-faced young guy leapt out and started screaming at us to get away from the runway. He kept shouting, 'Who the hell gave you permission to film here?' Our boss, a mild-mannered guy, couldn't get a word in edgeways. Eventually, the young chap settled down long enough for our boss to inform him that if we could not complete our job, Heathrow would lose its license to operate. He listened and realised he'd made a huge mistake (we'd also missed a pass by the CAFU aircraft whilst this went on—wasted fuel and time). Apparently the air traffic control watch had changed about an hour before and no one had told them we were on the runway. Mind you, it may have helped if our car had been standard black and yellow CAA colours. It was, in, fact orange and white.

Richard also had some nerve-wracking moments:

One night shift in the tower, I took a phone call from air traffic at about 3 a.m. to switch the ILS direction as an aircraft was coming straight in for an emergency landing. Because the airport was technically closed for the night, we only had a skeleton staff on duty. I was unable to get the equipment to respond from the control panel in the equipment room, and after much panic [I] had to admit defeat. The aircraft came in with no ILS and landed safely. It transpired there was a known fault that had prevented me switching over, but no one had told me. I thought it was down to my incompetence and I was for the high jump.

Heathrow never actually closes; it does have a 'first flight' and a 'last flight' of the day, but it is otherwise open twenty-four hours per day, seven days per week, fifty-two weeks per year. I asked Richard if he ever considered staying at Heathrow:

I went down a 'technical route' at school because, even at the tender age of sixteen, I could see that [it] was better for long-term employment, and so it proved. Being interested in aviation, the CAA offered a great mix for me. Later, it became clear that installation work across the UK for the CAA was much more lucrative and fun. Finally, when marriage loomed, I decided software was the future, so I joined the Digital Equipment Corporation and subsequently Compaq Computers and Hewlett Packard.

In 1973, Richard Briggs sits on what was the only security fencing around the airport at the time. (*Richard Briggs collection*)

15
Terminals

Terminals have always been, and probably always will be, the 'bottle-necks' of transportation, whether of ground, water, or air systems.

Harry H. Blee, US Aeronautics Branch, 1932

On 29 June 2015, Heathrow sent out a press release announcing the closure of Terminal 1:

—Heathrow Airport's Terminal 1 will close its doors after 47 years of operation
—Passengers now experiencing brand-new, world-class facilities in Terminal 2
—Heathrow now rated the best airport in Western Europe

Heathrow Terminal 1, opened by Queen Elizabeth II in May 1968, will say goodbye to its final passengers this evening. The terminal will close after 47 years with airlines having completed their move to new, modern world class facilities. The final departure will be a British Airways flight to Hanover, leaving on the evening of Monday June 29. British Airways (formally BEA) were also the first airline to operate from the terminal in 1968.

Since 2003, Heathrow has invested £11 billion in transforming Heathrow. Over the last year, the majority of flights have been moved from Terminal 1 to Terminal 2 and as a result, over 60% of Heathrow passengers will now experience new, world class facilities in Terminal 5 and Terminal 2. This was recognised at the 2015 World Airport Awards when Heathrow was awarded the 'Best Airport in Western Europe' by passengers.

The Terminal closure will make way for improved service and way finding around the airport and eventually an extension of the new Terminal 2 will take its place. If the Government supports a third runway at Heathrow then Terminal 2 will be extended farther, providing enough capacity to connect Britain to the world for the 21st century.

Terminal 1 was renowned for being the biggest short-haul terminal of its kind in Western Europe and handled approximately 9 million passengers at full capacity. In the last few weeks, the terminal has been home to just 17 flights and around 1,700 passengers a day as airlines were phased out of the Terminal.

Heathrow CEO John Holland Kaye said: 'The closure of Terminal 1 marks another important milestone in the transformation of Heathrow. Terminal 1 has served Britain well for nearly 50 years, but will soon make way for the expansion of Terminal 2, giving Britain a world class airport that we can all be proud of.'

Did you know:

—Terminal 1 became operational in May 1968 operating BEA, BKS Airlines, later to become Northeast, Autair [who changed their name in 1970, becoming Court Line] and Cambrian Airways domestic flights only.
—The first flight was BEA 5362 to Edinburgh.
—At the time of opening, Terminal 1 was the largest airport terminal in Europe.
—BEA operated a shuttle service to Glasgow which launched from Terminal 1—this was a service from which passengers could simply turn up and pay on board.
—Terminal 1 also operated their seat allocation at the gate using a complicated system which consisted of an aircraft seat map and stickers
—Judy Garland stubbed her toe in customs and subsequently turned the air blue
—The terminal operated BA Concorde charter flights—champagne specials which simply flew around the Bay of Biscay and back again

Heathrow's £11 billion investment has transformed Heathrow for passengers and included Terminal 5 A, B and C, a new control tower, a complete refurbishment of Terminals 3 and 4, and last year the new Terminal 2A and B. The opening of Terminal 5 in March 2008 created the opportunity to demolish the old building and make way for a modern terminal to replace Terminals 1 and 2. In future, Heathrow plans to extend Terminal 2 over the site of the existing Terminal 1. This will provide enough capacity to eventually replace Terminal 3. This is part of a complete transformation of Heathrow to provide passengers with World Class facilities, no matter which terminal they are travelling through.

TAM (Brazil) relocated from T1 in May, leaving BA the only airline to operate just 17 flights a day. Iceland Air left for T2 in March, and El Al left for T4 in April. When the terminal closes, BA's flights will be split between three and five. Terminal 1 has currently been operating predominantly short haul destinations from the terminal.

Closing T1 also marks the beginning of other crucial projects at Heathrow such as widening the taxiways on the north side of the airfield to facilitate A380s and improve punctuality, and installing a new generation of hold baggage screening.

Like other terminals, Terminal 1 held many memories for me, too, as I used it more than any other terminal. Granted, that aspect of T1's history matters little in the greater scheme of things, but it is nonetheless a matter of personal truth. When T1 is demolished, Heathrow will contain none of its original buildings in the former central area. The exception is the power station, which remains in the same place (for now, at least) it has always been, just south of the car park that overlooks T3's frontage. T3 itself will, at some point in the not-too-distant future, also vanish, and the Heathrow of the modern era will bear no resemblance to its original design. Once the Europa Building (Terminal 2), the Queen's Building next to it, and the original control tower had bitten the dust, and the new T2 The Queen's Terminal had risen from the broken bricks of the old, Heathrow's central area no longer had the diamond shape familiar to millions. The Heathrow known to Micky and Clive Martin, to Tony Horton and his father, and to my father and I was gone.

If he were alive today, my father—with or without a tie—would have looked in awe at the soaring spaces of the new T2 The Queen's Terminal, the cavernous interior of T5, and then determined that the old terminals were much nicer and more personal and very definitely less overpowering. With two parallel runways (and possibly eventually three), a linear arrangement of terminals, and remote satellite buildings where the aircraft park to disgorge their numbers, Heathrow will resemble Atlanta, along with several other airports around the world (old and new) that now have this shape.

More mature enthusiasts often mourn the way that the modern airliner follows the same basic formula no matter who the manufacturer is or the size of the aircraft. There is the fuselage, two wings with one engine on each (slung on pods below), a fin, and two short, stubby tail wings at the back. All aircraft are now the same, except for the venerable 747, which has been around in various versions for forty-seven years. The other exception is the new kid on the block, the Airbus A380—although truthfully it's not so new anymore. As of 2016 it has been in service for nearly a decade, albeit perhaps not in the numbers Airbus would like.

The short-haul Boeing 737 was the first of today's standard-shaped airliners. It's been around in various disguises for longer than the 747. Now, all aircraft look the same, and so do airport terminals. It is the most aerodynamically efficient and now basically standard design for an airliner, and airport terminal layouts have developed simultaneously.

The open spaces of Terminal 1 were once filled with check-in islands. (*Author*)

Terminal 1. Its low-roofed 1960s style looked dated by 2015. (*Author*)

Terminal 1 just before it closed; real people behind real check-in desks. (*Leo Martin*)

Terminal 1, soon to be gone, seen from its brand-new, temporary partner. The disused radar tower is on the left. (*Author*)

Heathrow's bus and coach station—still one of the country's largest. (*Author*)

With the demolition of the old T2, new bridges were built. (*Author*)

Inside one of the new bridges. (*Author*)

The Piccadilly Line, which runs from central London to Heathrow. (*Author*)

Heathrow Central Station; Terminals 1, 2, and 3 are served by this station. (*Author*)

Heathrow Central. (*Author*)

Getting to Terminal 5 means staying on the tube or switching trains. (*Author*)

Terminal 4 is served by a different train. (*Author*)

Terminal 1's narrow departures road demonstrated its outdated style in 2015. (*Author*)

The power station is now the only surviving original building in the central area. (*Author*)

Millions of people pass through them, reading a book or a newspaper, eating and drinking while waiting for their flight, and then going through security and a long corridor, often underground, to the gates, where identikit airliners wait to whisk them to another identikit building at the other end. To casual observers, the airport terminal is a very large space in which to process human cargo; when you've seen one, you've seen them all.

Can it be any other way? When the great railway station terminals were built (such as London's gothic fantasy of St Pancras, or the arched and sun-kissed windows of New York's Grand Central), they were backed by private companies and plenty of private money. The stations were grand and impressively large for their time (and some still are).

For the most part, airport terminals were not so grand, but there are always exceptions. Most early airport terminal designers made something of an architectural statement—sometimes at the behest of the airport owners, who were more often than not the local town council or city authority. At JFK, the terminals were owned and paid for by the airlines that used them. Eero Saarinen's TWA terminal was one of the most spectacular, and Pan Am's oval-shaped and glass-walled building was similarly stunning, with the airline's Boeing 707s and DC8s (unusually, Pan Am ordered both) parked underneath an overhanging roof umbrella to keep passengers dry if it was raining when they boarded. When American's terminal opened, it had the world's largest stained-glass and multi-coloured window as its eye-catching frontage. Only three of the original nine terminals now remain at JFK, TWA being one of them. British Airways is the second, although it has been much remodelled since it opened. Berlin Tempelhof was owned by the then-German government, so a statement was *de rigueur*—a loud declaration.

All the central area subways have been extensively remodelled since they were originally built.. (*Author*)

The newest subway leading to the equally new Terminal 2 The Queen's Terminal. (*Author*)

The now-closed T1 subway. (*Author*)

T3's subway. (*Author*)

Terminal 3's subway entrance. (*Author*)

Heathrow's Europa and Oceanic Buildings, both designed by Sir Frederick Gibberd, looked rather staid by comparison. Terminal 1 was always a low-roofed concrete box that was typical of the 1960s. It was nonetheless functional, but not especially attractive to look at—a trait shared by most other airport terminals from the same era. The designs depended on how much money was available, and in many cases there was often a tight budget and a brief to achieve the boldest possible design given the financial constraints. Not much has changed, even if the terminal designs have.

The same problem has applied to airports the world over, and it has been graphically demonstrated at Heathrow. None of the terminals were big enough as they were originally designed and built, and the space to expand them is limited by surrounding runways (as at New York's JFK). The scope for growth is at best severely restricted and at worst almost impossible.

In New York, those nine terminals around the oval-shaped central area were a reflection of the airlines that commissioned them—a cornucopia of different thoughts, systems, and regional and global aspirations. They were never meant to be part of a unified system through which passengers could move seamlessly from one connecting flight to the next. In fairness, the design thinking originated in an era where people went from one place to another and did not need to change airlines. The idea that one might need or want to go from their destination to another and then on somewhere else, changing airlines and thus terminals, was never a consideration.

All airports have to react to the demands placed on them, and almost all airports, with a few exceptions, have had to do so within existing boundaries—like Heathrow and New York.

The demands come from the airport's primary customers, the airlines that fly to them, who are, in turn, responding to the demands made by their customers—the ever-increasing numbers of passengers. However, it is rarely acknowledged that all airport authorities make often strenuous efforts to come up with redevelopment ideas that are financially workable and can be carried out with the minimum amount of disruption to passengers. People are always quick to complain (usually to the airlines) about delays even though it's rarely the fault or direct responsibility of the airlines themselves.

The JFK 2000 concept was an ambitious plan to construct a single new central terminal inside the ring of existing terminals, through which all arrivals and departures would move smoothly before a people mover system would whisk them to the individual airline terminals for their flights.

The neat title on the brochure promoting the project was 'Yesterday's Technology, Tomorrow's Demands'. It was produced by the Port Authority of New York and New Jersey to illustrate the revolution that would transform JFK from a sluggish, jam-packed, and truly inefficient way of handling people into a sleek, modern, efficient, and even pleasurable system. The plan floundered when JFK's airlines realised that the fees they would have to pay to the airport wold be gigantic.

All airlines pay to use an airport; there is a fee to land, a fee to take off, and a fee to park the aircraft while on the ground. While the terminals at JFK were owned by the airlines, the apron and its hardstands were still the property of the airport. The size of the fees usually depend on the size of the aircraft and how long it is on the ground (and, in more recent times, how much noise it makes). Having already paid large sums to build and develop terminals and subsequently cope with bigger aircraft, then to redevelop those same terminals, JFK's airlines shied away from being made to pay huge new fees for the huge new central terminal building—especially one over which they would have no control.

The JFK 2000 plan never moved on from the brochure stage. Sixteen years on from when it was supposed to be a reality, just two of JFK's original nine terminals are still in use. The much-changed British Airways terminal still stands, along with the one originally built for the long-gone Braniff (today it is imaginatively called 'Terminal 2' and used for Delta's domestic flights). Terminal 2 will also go at some point, being replaced by a new and more efficient design. The TWA terminal is no longer used, although it still stands as a preserved historic structure. At the time of writing, various ideas for the future purpose of the building have been proposed and refused; the latest is a plan to convert the building into part of a new hotel that includes a 10,000-square-foot observation deck alongside 500 guest rooms and 40,000 square feet of conference, event, and meeting space. A 10,000-square-foot observation deck would certainly regenerate enthusiasm. JFK now has big new terminals, although there no longer nine of them. There are six, all still located within the central area; they are bigger (except for Terminal 2) and make better use of the space available.

At Heathrow, it's a little different. There has never been a single, comprehensive rebuild of the whole site (as the JFK 2000 plan proposed). There has never been the political will to say, 'We got it wrong—albeit understandably—when Heathrow was designed and built, so let's really get hold of it now and rebuild it all, and let's not hang about. Let's get the job done.' If there has ever been a plan like this, the public have never been told about it, which would hardly be surprising given the furore that would have ensued.

However, there is something similar now planned at New York's second airport, La Guardia (LGA). It was built and opened in 1939, bursting at the seams almost from the first day the flights used its runways (much like Heathrow). La Guardia's current terminal opened in 1964 and has barely changed since. It's old and too small—particularly for the bigger aircraft of today. Eastern and Delta subsequently opened their own terminals at the eastern end the airport, some distance from the main terminal, giving LGA a similar problem to JFK. Changing airlines and terminals was a nightmare. At Heathrow, even after T4 opened, changing terminals was mostly relatively painless, but this was not the case at either of the airports in New York. On Monday 27 July 2015, Governor of New York Andrew Cuomo and US Vice President Joe Biden announced a $4 billion construction project for La Guardia. It involves the complete demolition of the existing, outdated terminals and their replacement by a single, much larger terminal.

Aircraft will park at gates at remote islands set in front of the main building, like Heathrow's T5 and new T2. Unlike at Heathrow's T2 and T5, the gates will be reached by passenger bridges high enough for aircraft to taxi underneath. Gatwick's north terminal has one of these bridges, as does Denver. They have the benefit of allowing daylight to reach inside, not burrowing under the apron, a good view, and of being cheaper than tunnels. The La Guardia project is expected to break ground in 2016, with the majority of the first half of the new area expected to be open to passengers in 2019. Full completion of the project is scheduled for approximately eighteen months later. The entire redevelopment will take just five years to complete (2016–2021) and will be finished ten years before Heathrow builds its new runway—if it does.

Compare, if you will, the time taken to build Heathrow's Terminal 5. This took over a decade and a half of planning, discussions, protests, inquiries, more discussions, more protests, continuing inquiries, and, eventually, construction. T5 was formally announced in May 1992, BAA submitting a planning application in February 1993.

A public enquiry began over two years later at Heathrow's Renaissance Hotel, continuing for almost four years. The enquiry eventually came to an end on 17 March 1999, after sitting for a remarkable 525 days. More than eight years after the initial planning application had been made, then-transport minister Stephen Byers granted permission for the terminal's construction. Terminal 5 opened for business on 27 March 2008, sixteen years after it was announced.

Granted, it has taken New York a very long time to get around to the redevelopment (largely as a result of money issues), but having finally bitten the proverbial bullet, the transformation of both JFK and LGA will take a lot less time than it will take Heathrow to build one new runway. Their progress is even more remarkable when considering the fact that most of the New York improvements have taken place since 9/11.

Heathrow is not alone in its struggles to cope with ever-rising passenger numbers and the ever-larger aircraft carrying them, but it seems to be a uniquely British trait to ponder the possible solutions and then continue to do nothing. Heathrow's first terminal, the Europa Building, was expanded by the addition of two airside piers, extending out over the ramp. To begin with, just sixteen aircraft (BEA's and everybody else's) could park nose-in, with eight contact gates on each pier, four along each side (although the gates initially did not have airbridges). The Oceanic Building took all the long-haul flights

Lower left: the bus and coach station. Upper left: Terminal 1. Right: the giant new Terminal 2. Centre right: the grassy hump is all that remains of the original control tower. (*Author*)

Terminal 2, The Queen's Terminal, with it cavernous entry area. (*Author*)

from the overcrowded and cramped north side to its new location in the central area, and Terminal 1 was built, meaning sixteen aircraft from the European airlines that served Heathrow could then use the two piers at the now-renamed Terminal 2.

The number of aircraft accommodated dropped even further when the wide-bodied A300 came into service. The terminal could ultimately only handle twelve aircraft, using contact gates, now complete with airbridges, at the piers. The rest were dispersed to remote parking, meaning a bus journey for passengers travelling to and from their aircraft. Some relief was felt when the Eurolounge was opened on some of the remote parking stands between Terminals 1 and 2. A boxy building linked to both terminals, it was used predominantly by passengers travelling to Brussels, Amsterdam, and especially Paris (London–Paris was still the busiest international air route at the time). Some years later, a long pier was added further airside, meaning the remote stands beyond the Eurolounge were brought closer and made into contact gates with airbridges.

Runways had long been withdrawn from use and paved over to significantly enlarge the parking areas for aircraft, meaning that Terminal 1's piers stretched out into the distance. The typical scenes in the 1970s, '80s, and '90s saw a long row of BEA Tridents and BAC111s morph into a long row of British Airways Tridents and BAC111s. They were eventually replaced by equally long rows of Boeing 737s and 757s, with the wide-bodied Lockheed TriStar taking up the space where two smaller aircraft would once have been handled. T1's longest pier, the one used for international flights, was very long, and it took a while to walk from the terminal itself to the gate if one's aircraft was parked at the far end, not too far from the threshold of 27 right. The domestic pier was less than half as long. When my father and I went to Jersey and I loaded the bags, the Vickers Viscount that took us was at the farthest gate from the terminal, but it took no time to get to it, so those who loaded the aircraft were in good shape.

Over in Terminal 3, the extension for the 747 was built—the pier connecting the terminal to the cross-pier and its gates, where the bloated shape of the 747 would actually be found. Moving walkways were also installed, which were handy at the end of a journey from the distant and exotic cities of the world. Similar moving walkways were found in the subterranean passages from the London Underground station that served the three terminals. They're still there—for now.

One tumbles off the rattling tube train and spends some time deep beneath the bustling surface of the airport above, taking the moving walkway to the terminal you want to reach. Today, at least in the central area, those passageways will only take you to T3 and the new T2 The Queen's Terminal. To get to T4 or T5 means taking a train.

Heathrow has plodded along, an addition here, an addition there, with no grand master plan, no equivalent of JFK 2000. It is a testimony to the airport and the airlines, along with those who work there, that Heathrow has continued to successfully move the millions of passengers through its eventually cramped three central-area terminals. It is a miracle that T1, T2, and T3 served as well as they did for so long; something eventually had to give. The Europa Building is gone, T1 is gone, and T3 will go. Their replacements may look similar to the other new terminals around the world (and perhaps to each other, at least inside), but Heathrow's new buildings are as eye-catching as they come.

The London Underground will get you from the city to the airport in around fifty minutes (depending on the terminal), while the more recent Heathrow Express train

Aviators at Terminal 3. (*Author*)

Between its car park and the terminal itself, the new T2's open spaces could give a good view of Terminal 4 and runway 27 left/09 right. The lack of a spectator's viewing deck is something of a missed opportunity. (*Author*)

THIS STONE WAS UNVEILED BY
HER MAJESTY
QUEEN ELIZABETH II
TO MARK THE FORMAL
INAUGURATION OF THE
CENTRAL TERMINAL AREA
16TH DECEMBER 1955

The surviving artefact. (*Author*)

Compare the landside interior of 2015's T2 with its predecessor from 1955. (*Author*)

The new terminal's landside arrivals. (*Author*)

Terminal 3. Again, the difference between 1961 and 2015 is quite marked. (*Author*)

Its days may be numbered, but T3's modernity makes it look spacious. (*Author*)

Terminal 3 departures. (*Author*)

Terminal 3 arrivals. (*Author*)

from Paddington Station will take around fifteen minutes, but it's more expensive to use. Arriving at Terminal 5's gleaming modernity, the journey from the station platform takes the unwary through imposingly skeletal and broodingly massive frames of supporting columns and beams, up the escalators, until daylight finally beckons.

Terminal 5 is home to British Airways, and its red, white, and blue is everywhere. Like almost every other modern airport, there are rows of self-service check-in machines, and beyond them are real people behind real check-in desks. If your flight is using one of the gates that adjoin the airside frontage—known as Terminal 5A—you don't have far to go, but many flights use one of the two remote satellites. If your flight departs from one of these gates, you will need to dive back underground and use the Bombardier Innovia APM 200 automated people-mover system to transport oneself between T5A, T5B, and T5C.

At the time of writing, I have not used T5 yet. I have also not used the new T2 (which follows the same concept) as a passenger. However, I have been inside both terminals for a wander and an enquiring look. The same remarkable vista waits for the uninitiated traveller at the new T2. Like its slightly older cousin, the new terminal's size can be a little overpowering. There is an equally overpowering sculpture looming over the landside of the terminal, but it can actually be missed by anybody intent on simply getting to check-in and their flight. It is named *Slipstream* and weighs 77 tonnes, with a length of 78 metres. Created by sculptor Richard Wilson, Slipstream cost £2.5 million to make; it now hangs above the masses entering and leaving. Its waving shape runs across the roof, suspended above the terminal's users, but its length can detract from the purpose of the building. Arriving passengers simply want to get out of the airport and go home, or to their business meeting or hotel.

Terminal 5's construction can seem almost ominous. (*Author*)

Columns of steel. (*Author*)

Emerging from the netherworld. (*Author*)

Above: In places, Terminal 5 can seem almost ghostly. (*Author*)

Below: Terminal 5 landside arrivals. (*Author*)

Terminal 5 landside departures. (*Author*)

Terminal 5's construction is reminiscent of the days of propeller-driven airliners. (*Author*)

It took a long time, but British Airways finally gained exclusive use of a single terminal. (*Author*)

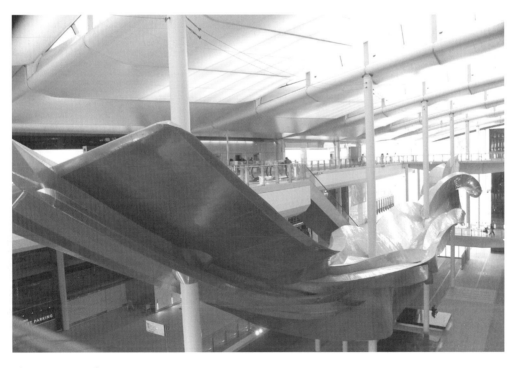

Slipstream. (*Author*)

The sculpture is intended to be a solid representation of the shape carved in the air by a stunt plane. This, in combination with its material (riveted aluminium), serves to remind people of the aeronautics of the past. In an era of wide-bodied flying, mass travel, and jet airliners that power their way skywards and beyond, is a reminder of the past a reassurance, or something else? It depends on the passenger. There are plenty of people who do not like flying and will not enjoy looking at *Slipstream*.

The new Terminal 2, The Queen's Terminal, cost £2.5 billion to build. It might look similar to most new terminals across the world, but it will serve the airport well—unless you're an enthusiast.

With the café just inside the terminal on the right, the end of the departure roadway is another missed opportunity to provide a supervised and secure location for spotters. (*Author*)

Above: Some photography is just about possible. (*Author*)

Opposite above: Café Nero has become a favoured place for spotters, offering a good view of aircraft landing on runway 09 left. (*Author*)

Opposite below: However, photography from the café is a little problematic. (*Author*)

Peace and serenity; the inner courtyard between T5's car park and the terminal. (*Author*)

The courtyard's dancing fountains. (*Author*)

16

Runways

Air travel reminds us who we are. It's the means by which we recognize ourselves as modern.

Don DeLillo

There is an unavoidable problem with writing books about airports; aviation (and particularly commercial aviation) is characterised by an ever-changing fluidity of new aircraft, new routes, old routes, dropped routes, reinstated routes, retired old aircraft and retired new aircraft, and rising numbers and descending numbers. New airlines start, fail, start again, and fail again. Names change as one airline buys out another, gets bought out itself, and successive new ownerships change the name yet again. Long-established and great names of the airline industry lumber along seemingly forever and then come tumbling down, as happened with Pan Am. Others carry on regardless.

Although terminals and runway layouts can seem outwardly similar for years and decades, the changes wrought by bigger aircraft and new requirements mean there are at least internal changes at airports year by year—and especially at Heathrow. 'Alterations as usual during business…' This also means that by the time you read these words, they will be out of date.

Wednesday 1 July 2015

The Airports Commission, led by Sir Howard Davies, was set up to decide where another runway in the south east of England could be built. It deliberated for more than two years. London Mayor Boris Johnson (who is stepping down in 2016) became the Member of Parliament for Uxbridge, a little way to the north west of Heathrow, in May 2015. He had been one of the prime supporters of building a new airport on reclaimed land in the Thames Estuary, not too far from Southend. The concept became known as 'Boris Island'. Another proposal was to build a brand new airport on the north-Kent coast, on the Isle of Sheppey, more or less opposite Southend, which lies on the other side of the estuary. Both would have been prohibitively expensive and both were discounted by the commission on that basis.

This was not the first time that someone had suggested building a new airport for London. In 1971, the Conservative government announced its intention to ensure an end to further growth at both Heathrow and Gatwick and close Stansted altogether. A new super-airport was to be built on land reclaimed from the sea at Maplin Sands, at a place known as Foulness, off the Essex coast. The airport's location would, in all probability, have also meant the closure of nearby Southend Airport. In recent years, Southend has rebranded itself as 'London Southend' and had its runway extended in order to attract more traffic—a move seemingly approved by the people of the town.

Planned to open in 1980, Maplin Sands (or Foulness, if you prefer) would have had four runways and a capacity of 125 million passengers per year. With aircraft approach and departure routes over water, noise would not be an issue. As with the later idea of a new airport on the north Kent coast, environmental and ecological objections were raised, but it was financial considerations that spelt the end of the plan, with the newly elected Labour government of 1974 cancelling the project.

Meanwhile, passenger numbers and aircraft movements continued to rise. Forty years on, with political expediency and general dithering dominant, there was still no additional runway capacity in one of the busiest areas of the commercial aviation world.

Sir Howard and his colleagues narrowed the choice to just three options. Heathrow had two—an extra runway built north and west of the Bath Road, or the more than doubling of the length of the existing Runway No. 1 (09 left/27 right), with the idea being that one half would be for take-offs and the other for landings. The third option was a second runway at Gatwick. In all three cases, the plan is for the runway to become operational some fifteen years after the final decision.

Sir Howard announced the commission's recommendation that a brand-new runway should be built at Heathrow, north and west of the Bath Road. The government announced that it would make a decision based on the findings at the end of 2015, but they have delayed this announcement.

There is always an instant reaction from all and sundry to such recommendations; these reactions are often inaccurate and ill-informed and often come from those with a vested interest. Predictably, immediate objections arose from Conservative MPs who have constituencies around Heathrow. There were additional howls of anguish from the anti-Heathrow folks and whoops of glee from the anti-Gatwick people.

On the day of the commission's announcement, London Mayor Boris Johnson gave an interview to the BBC, commenting that such decisions were made 'in the 1950s, perhaps, but not today'. He was probably unaware that Amsterdam, Paris, and Frankfurt have all built new runways within the last few years (the German airport being the most recent). Yet the new runway at Heathrow will not be open for another fifteen years. If it is built, it's a fair bet that at least one other European airport will open additional runways before Heathrow does.

The three continental airports mentioned above are all cited as Heathrow's competitors, but Heathrow does not compete with any airport other than Gatwick, and it only does that by virtue of the short-sighted decision to hive off airports from what used to be BAA. The two airports serve different markets and should perfectly complement each other, but this would only be possible if the UK had a joined-up commercial aviation policy instead of decades of countless politicians using the emotive nature of the subject to gain votes.

The little ones come too. Romania's Tarom airline currently operates the Airbus A318, the smallest of the Airbus narrow-bodied family. (*Author*)

American Airlines, a major user of LHR since the acquisition of TWA's Heathrow routes in May 1991—the same year Pan Am sold its Heathrow routes to United. (*Author*)

Airbus A340, Manila to London. (*Author*)

An Airbus A340 coming in from Colombo. (*Author*)

Vueling.com, now operating many of Iberia's services from Spain. (*Author*)

The Boeing 747 is becoming a rare sight except when used by British Airways. Cathay Pacific's cargo haulers are another exception. (*Author*)

Welcome back. G-BIKK, a Boeing 757-236, once flew in and out of Heathrow several times a day for British Airways and its passengers; now it carries cargo for DHL. (*Author*)

Iberia's new colours. The Spanish flag-carrier still maintains daily links to Madrid and is part of the International Airlines Group (IAG), which includes British Airways. (*Author*)

Scandinavian Airlines System (SAS) are another major operator at Heathrow. (*Author*)

Air France are another long-standing user of the airport. (*Author*)

The Dutch national carrier's subsidiary, KLM Cityhopper, operates one of the smallest aircraft to use Heathrow—the Brazilian-built Embraer 195. (*Author*)

Airlines are businesses and thus have to make money. They want to serve the airport that is most appealing to their customers, which is Heathrow—not Gatwick or any other airport masquerading as a London airport, whether it is London Southend, London Luton, London Oxford, or London Ashford. All four airports have added the capital's name to their own in order to attract additional business. In the case of Oxford and Ashford, they are attempting to gain 'business' business. All except Luton are over an hour by train from London itself, and the road journeys are even more time-consuming. The same applies to London Birmingham and London Manchester, an hour and a half and two hours (or more) respectively from central London by train. The trains are often packed, meaning some of those who want to travel between London, Birmingham, and Manchester have standing room only and nowhere near enough space for their bags. I have travelled both routes several times, squeezing my way onto the overloaded trains; flying is a much more civilised way to go.

People travel to Amsterdam, Frankfurt, or Paris because they want to go to Amsterdam, Frankfurt, or Paris. They fly to London because they want to go to London, and they do not want to have to make a 200-mile road, train and/or sea journey at the end of the flight. Think back to 1946—airlines forced to use Bournemouth Hurn demanded to use the then-still-under-construction Heathrow because of the lengthy and uncomfortable road journey passengers had to take in order to get to their final destination.

At one stage, Amsterdam's airport ran an advertising campaign billing itself as 'London's Fifth Airport', despite there being a large chunk of the North Sea between the Netherlands and the UK. They did this because it receives more direct flights from UK airports than Heathrow ever has. The campaign was aimed at people in places like Birmingham and

BA's main UK competitor, Virgin Atlantic. Its Airbus A340 aircraft are being retired in favour of new Boeing 787 Dreamliners. (*Author*)

The other small one. Brussels Airlines, the successor to bankrupt Sabena, operate the British-built BAe 146 on the short hop from Belgium. (*Author*)

In an often unpredictably volatile industry, mighty Lufthansa is one of the most stable airlines in the world. (*Author*)

Morocco's national airline. (*Author*)

Norwich, or other major urban areas that did not have flights to Heathrow, enabling potential passengers to connect at Amsterdam to KLM's worldwide network.

Expanding either Heathrow or Gatwick will generate jobs for people. For this reason alone, the case for the expansion of Heathrow is unanswerable; just over 6,000 jobs would be created by the expansion of Gatwick, but nearly 80,000 would be created at Heathrow.

One of the biggest misnomers in the airport world is the terminology used to describe the size of an airport, with even those who work in the industry being guilty of adding to the confusion. There is talk of airports 'getting larger', and how fast an airport is 'growing'. The general public, and especially those immovably opposed to any airport expansions, take this to mean that an airport is getting physically bigger. What is actually meant is that airports get busier. In its seventy years of existence, Heathrow has never increased in physical or geographical size. Other than the extension of the two present runways to the west (which was provided for in the original plans), the only way in which the airport was increased in terms of land area was the building of Terminal 5. However, T5 was built on the sewage works in between the western ends of the two main runways. Nevertheless, the incredibly short-sighted and yet politically expedient (at the time) decision not to build the three extra runways north of the Bath Road (as provided for in the original plans) now looks like the kind of political manoeuvring that today results in politicians facing strident demands to resign. Then again, the same could be said for the method used to get Heathrow built to begin with.

When (or if) Heathrow gets its new runway, the little village of Longford, just north of T5 on the other side of runway 09 left's threshold, will vanish. The impact on the village of Sipson in the 1950s would have been far greater, as it too would have been demolished it its entirety. The new plan puts the runway further west and leaves Sipson almost untouched. One has to wonder how many people were alive back in 1947, when the first plans for Heathrow were revealed, and who are still alive today, living in the same houses. There are probably not many; still, if you buy a house near an airport, you must live with the possible consequences. Curiously, much of the land between Heathrow's existing northern boundary and the M4 motorway is still open and vacant, left that way for the airport to grow. Most of it is owned by Heathrow Airport.

This doesn't help the village of Longford, or, for that matter, Harmondsworth, half of which will also be demolished. There will be a wave of protests, demonstrations, and more arguments, and yet some of those protesters will no doubt be getting on a plane at some point, going somewhere for their holidays, complaining bitterly about the delays.

There are lies, damned lies and statistics. Statistics can be made to mean anything, depending on who is using them. Those totally opposed to airport expansion will use statistics to demonstrate why a new runway should not be built anywhere. On the day the Airports Commission released its recommendation, the Campaign to Protect Rural England (CPRE) immediately issued a press release:

Third Heathrow Runway would be Full Frontal Assault on Green Belt and Tranquillity

Wednesday, 01 July 2015 08:15

Inevitably, Aer Lingus are also a big player at Heathrow. (*Author*)

Inbound from Helsinki, another Airbus narrow-body. (*Author*)

Unusually for a European airline, Poland's LOT fly Boeings instead of Airbus aircraft (KLM are the other notable exception). (*Author*)

An Air Malta Airbus A320. (*Author*)

The Airports Commission's flawed terms of reference meant its recommendation of a destructive new runway was inevitable, say rural campaigners. The Campaign to Protect Rural England (CPRE) condemned today's decision of the Airports Commission to recommend a third runway at Heathrow.

If it is ever built, the proposed Heathrow north western runway would be expected to:

- Destroy 694 hectares of Green Belt and 60 hectares of woodland;
- Wreck tranquillity in parks and gardens with impacts likely to spread into the Chilterns Area of Outstanding Natural Beauty;
- Destroy up to 950 homes and require up to 70,800 new homes to be built by 2030, with many more being required afterwards – all in an area of acute housing pressure;
- Produce 54.6% of the UK's aviation carbon emissions in 2050.

Ralph Smyth, the transport campaign manager at the Campaign to Protect Rural England (CPRE), commented:

The recommendation today for a third runway at Heathrow casts a dark shadow over a wide swathe of the south east. Besides the destruction of much of the ancient village of Harmondsworth to make way for the new runway, a much wider area is at threat. On top of the almost relentless din of jet engines, runaway development and traffic would shatter the remaining fragments of tranquil countryside in the south east, already one of the most densely over flown areas in the world.

All of the options short-listed by the Airports Commission would have a devastating impact on the countryside, directly as well as indirectly. But, equally, they would undermine the national imperative of rebalancing our economy away from the overheated south east. London already has 50% more flights to it than any other city in the world and enough's enough. We believe that the growing political consensus over the need for a Northern Powerhouse will effectively pull the rug from under the Commission's report. We now need a national spatial plan to rebalance growth and aviation, making the most of the ample spare capacity in other airports.

While the Airports Commission in some ways set new standards for public engagement, it was clear that its terms of reference were rigged from the start. Another new runway in the south east was the foregone conclusion, preventing proper consideration of greater use of high speed rail or an ambitious regional rebalancing strategy.

The release carried the following notation at its end:

The Campaign to Protect Rural England (CPRE) fights for a better future for the English countryside. We work locally and nationally to protect, shape and enhance a beautiful, thriving countryside for everyone to value and enjoy. Our members are united in their love for England's landscapes and rural communities, and stand up for the countryside, so it can continue to sustain, enchant and inspire future generations. Founded in 1926, President: Sir Andrew Motion, Patron: Her Majesty The Queen.

The CPRE also stated that all its figures were taken from the Airports Commission report. The alacrity with which this release was issued suggests that the CPRE was ready to fire it off, expecting the recommendation to be for Heathrow. It does not say why the CPRE considers the commission's terms of reference to be have been 'rigged', and the reference to (and presumably enthusiasm for) high-speed rail links is something of a contradiction to the not terribly dissimilar protests regarding the proposed new high-speed rail link the government wants to build running north from London. It is true that much of Harmondsworth will be demolished, but interestingly, it would have been almost untouched if the original plan had been followed as suggested by the layout panel report in 1947. There is no mention of Longford or the amount of empty land immediately north of the airport; the wishes of airline customers to go to London and not anywhere else is also ignored, as is the demand on already overcrowded trains. The release does not specify which parks will be adversely affected, and it does not say what the impact will be in on the Chilterns, which are further west and regularly over-flown now—including by aircraft using Oxford's airport. The comments regarding the Northern Powerhouse and the 'ample spare capacity' at other airports ignore the fact that people who want to go to London want to be able to actually go to London. The CPRE also demonstrate some economy with the facts when they state 'London already has 50% more flights to it than any other city in the world'. Heathrow is not the busiest airport in the world, nor has it ever been; until recently, it was the busiest international airport, but not the busiest overall.

On the other hand, there are some facts that cannot be avoided, no matter how one chooses to present them. The source can be either considered authoritative or taken with the proverbial pinch of salt, but it's not unreasonable to assume that Britain's Civil Aviation Authority (CAA) can be relied upon. In a press release dated 24 July 2015, the CAA stated:

Record passenger numbers highlights strong demand for air travel

- The most passengers at UK airports, including those on the Isle of Man and the Channel Islands in the first quarter of any year since the start of the global financial crisis
- Strongest passenger growth of any quarter in the last 10 years (This is with exception of Q2 2011. This quarter followed Iceland's volcanic eruption in April and May 2010, which severely affected air traffic/passenger travel in Q2 2010).
- Highest rolling 12 month passenger total since records began.

UK airports have seen the strongest start to a year since 2008—with first quarter passenger numbers now close to levels which were last seen during the pre-recession years.

Between January and March 2015, UK terminals handled 50.2m passengers, making this year's Q1 the busiest since the same period in 2008, just prior to the global financial crisis, which accounted for 51.4m passengers.

The first three months of 2015 also recorded the largest growth in passenger numbers (7.5 per cent) of any quarter in the last 10 years. Figures show this increase was primarily the result of growth in European traffic (nine per cent) and domestic traffic (seven per cent).

Another relatively new kid on the block. (*Author*)

Most of Air India's flights to Heathrow are now operated by the new Boeing 787 Dreamliner. (*Author*)

The Hobbit. Air New Zealand have created almost a trademark look by painting Lord of the Rings images on their aircraft.

Jet Airways are Air India's main competitor today. (*Author*)

Commercial flights for Q1 2015 have also increased (471,000) showing the strongest growth (2.9 per cent) of any quarter for nine years, since Q1 2006.

These strong growth figures are revealed in the CAA's latest quarterly Aviation Trends report, which provides detailed analysis of the UK aviation industry.

Rolling 12 months

The strong start to the year has also helped UK airports record the best rolling 12 month passenger number total since records began.

In the last four quarters 243.9m passengers departed and arrived at all reporting UK airports. This surpasses the previous rolling 12 month peak of 243.3m passengers, between Q2 2007 and Q1 2008 (April 2007 to March 2008).

These numbers also mean passenger demand across a 12 month period has, for the first time, surpassed the levels last witnessed before the 2008 financial crisis and subsequent UK recession.

In this same 12 month period the number of passenger flights across UK airports has increased by 1.3 per cent to 2m. In this period London airports showed a 3.6 per cent rise to 1.02m, though regional airports recorded a dip of 1.1 per cent to 977,000.

Punctuality

On-time performance of scheduled passenger flights in Q1 2015 at all UK airports fell or remained unchanged when compared with Q1 2014. London airports dropped from 84 per cent in Q1 2014 to 80 per cent in Q1 2015. Regional airports dropped from 86 per cent to 81 per cent. Overall on-time performance at all UK airports dropped from 85 per cent to 80 per cent.

Average delay of scheduled passenger flights in Q1 2015 increased at all airports with the exception of Jersey and Bournemouth, which saw average delay fall by two minutes and one minute respectively against Q1 2014. Average delay at all London airports increased by two minutes from 10 to 12 minutes. Regional airports increased from nine minutes to 11 minutes. For all UK airports average delay increased by two minutes from nine minutes to 11 minutes in Q1 2014/2015.

Tim Johnson, CAA Policy Director, said: 'The large increase in first quarter passenger numbers has led to UK airports recording their busiest ever 12 months and means that for the first time air travel has exceeded the levels last seen before the 2008 financial crisis.

'Figures also show commercial flight numbers are growing much faster at London airports than elsewhere which highlights the pressures both on runway capacity and airspace in the South East. The increasing levels of air travel highlights the importance of addressing these two issues. Without changes both to infrastructure on the ground and in the air, consumers will face higher charges, less choice and more disruption.'

This is heavy stuff. Tim Johnson's comment about more disruption suggests increased delays, so a new runway will have to be built somewhere.

Is one really enough? One of the comments made by Sir Howard's Commission is that no fourth runway should be built at Heathrow and that the government should legislate to ensure that a fourth can never be built. This is as short-sighted as the decision not to build the three north of the Bath Road to begin with, or even not to build a new airport at Maplin Sands. Bearing that in mind, one of the more significant aspects to Sir Howard's work is a comment made regarding what happens after a new runway is built 'by 2030', the date by which a third runway at Heathrow or a second at Gatwick will be needed. Sir Howard has stated that on top of the new runway on which his commission has deliberated, another will be needed by 2050—although he also made clear that that choice is beyond the remit of the current process. This is something of a contradiction to the remarks concerning not building a fourth at Heathrow.

Leaving aside the question as to why fifteen years must pass before a runway is built, and the fact that a fourth will be needed another fifteen years beyond that, the real issue is not whether Heathrow needs a third runway or not. It doesn't—it needs two.

Heathrow needs both a third and a fourth runway and it needs them now—not in fifteen or thirty years. Gatwick has a strong case for the immediate construction of a second runway in addition to two more at Heathrow. Commencing work on three runways now would do a number of things; it would make both airports more robust in their ability to handle runway closures, especially in winter; it would, to a degree, future-proof both airports' needs for some years to come; and it would enable both airports to compete more effectively with each other. The reasons are not merely to do with competitiveness. The runways are needed to ensure both airports run more efficiently and more safely, and they are needed now.

In December 2015, the government announced that the seventy-year-old tradition of dithering over Heathrow and other UK airports would continue, delaying their final decision over a new runway until some time in the summer of 2016. The reason given was to allow further time for studies into the environmental impact of a third runway at Heathrow. Many observers have looked, laughed, and concluded that the delay has little to do with the environment; any such impact will be the same whether it is a new runway at Heathrow or at Gatwick.

The Conservative MP for Richmond is Zac Goldsmith. His constituency lies a little way to the east of Heathrow and under the approach paths to the airport. He is an implacable opponent of a third runway and has suggested that he will resign as an MP if a new runway is approved. He is also the Conservative candidate for Mayor of London, aiming to replace fellow Conservative Boris Johnson, who stands down as Mayor in 2016 and who is also an opponent of the expansion of Heathrow. With the mayoral election looming on 5 May 2016, the Conservative government does not want to undermine Goldsmith's campaign by forcing him to oppose the government's position on expansion.

Interestingly, when David Cameron was leader of the opposition, he made an announcement prior to the 2010 general election in which he stated, 'No ifs, no buts, no third runway.' Cameron made his announcement in Richmond—Zac Goldsmith's constituency. Think back to December 1952, when the government of the day announced that the originally planned third triangle of runways would not be built, despite the land already

Watching either a Boeing 747 or Airbus 380 emerge through early morning mist can be a little eerie. (*Author*)

British Airway's Boeing 767-336 fleet are slowly being withdrawn from use and replaced by new Boeing 787s. (*Author*)

One of the replacement Boeing 787s. (*Author*)

Several of BA's Airbus A319s (such as G-EUPG, pictured here) were painted in special colours for the 2012 Olympics in London. (*Author*)

being acquired. Today, for the most part, this land has been left open and undeveloped, and it is owned by Heathrow Airport. Sixty-three years on, nothing has changed.

Predictably, those who oppose expansion at Gatwick have already added their voices to the maelstrom, and business leaders, along with news media, have slated the government for the delay. One of those business leaders is British Airways boss Willie Walsh.

BA are one of three airlines in the International Airlines Group (IAG), of which Walsh is also the Chief Executive Officer. At one point, Walsh suggested that no government would have the courage to build a third runway at Heathrow. In a newspaper article on Tuesday 15 December 2015, Walsh stated that he would move his business to Dublin, where the Irish airline Aer Lingus is based, or to Madrid, where Iberia is based. The two airlines are the other members of the IAG.

What does Walsh actually mean when he says he will 'move [his] business elsewhere'? To the general public, it means that British Airways are leaving Heathrow. Dublin is a non-starter; it is smaller than Heathrow by some distance, and BA simply would not fit. The Irish airport is unlikely to ever have the capacity to handle such a huge increase in the number of flights BA would bring. Madrid's Barajas Airport, on the other hand, underwent a huge increase in size from the 1990s to 2004, when it gained new terminals and (significantly) runways. Still, it probably could not handle BA's operations in addition to Iberia's. In all probability, Walsh was suggesting a shrinking of BA's business at Heathrow.

Who wants to go to Madrid in order to get to New York, or from London to Moscow via Spain? Who, for that matter, wants to go anywhere west, north, or east of London? One might conceivably agree to changing aircraft at Madrid if going on to China, Japan, or Australia, but carriers from those regions will still serve Heathrow. The only loser from a reduction of BA flights to Heathrow would be BA.

The fact remains that in order to operate safely and efficiently, Heathrow still needs two new runways and Gatwick still needs one. There has been no increase in runway capacity in the south east of England since the end of the Second World War. The last new construction of airport runway infrastructure was when Heathrow Airport itself was actually built.

The United Kingdom has given so much to the world—such as the invention of the jet engine, the primary cause of much of the furore over airport expansion—but the country's innovative spirit has never been limited solely to aviation. It needs to make up its mind about what it wants to be. The UK could be a place where its innovations are maintained and improved, solidifying its reputation as a country to visit and do business in, or it could be a country that stands and watches as the rest of the world speeds by.

An early-morning Airbus. (*Author*)

The longest of the Airbus narrow-bodied types is the A321. (*Author*)

One of Europe's fastest-growing airlines is Turkey's THY, which operates both Boeing and Airbus products; this image shows one of the airlines' Airbus A330s. (*Author*)

Vienna calling… (*Author*)

The space next to the approach lights over the Great Southwest Road is good for close-ups, but it is a little noisy—even with today's quieter aircraft. (*Author*)

Late afternoon reflections on a Tunis Air A320. (*Author*)

Terminal 4 landside arrivals. (*Author*)

The unrestricted view on the approach road to T4 is now just a memory. (*Author*)

17
Domesticity and Connectivity

My soul is in the sky.

William Shakespeare, *A Midsummer Night's Dream*, Act V, Scene I

If you have already visited London from outside the UK, then you probably used Heathrow. If your flight was with a low-fare airline, you would have used Gatwick or Stansted. It's not impossible you entered the UK at Birmingham or Manchester, or even at some other UK airport, and got to London by train or even on a bus so good luck with that. There are some twenty-four airports around the UK that are capable of handling flights to most European destinations, including holiday resorts in countries around the Mediterranean, which is where many of the UK's regional airports get much of their business. Aberdeen, Belfast, Edinburgh, Glasgow, Inverness, Leeds/Bradford, Ronaldsway on the Isle of Man, the Channel Islands of Jersey and Guernsey, Newcastle, Liverpool, and Manchester all have direct flights to and from at least one of the London airports.

There are four—Heathrow, Gatwick, Stansted, and London City—not counting those other airports in the south east of England, further away, that have stuck 'London' onto their name to attract flights, like Luton and Southend. Low-fare airlines operate most of the services, and as a result, flying can be cheaper than the equivalent rail fares. Flybe, EasyJet, and Ryanair are the principal low-fare carriers operating domestically, and none serve Heathrow. The three airline's flights are spread across three airports; Ryanair and Flybe use Stansted, which has a fraction of the flights serving Heathrow, and EasyJet uses both Gatwick and Luton.

It used to be different. At one time, Heathrow had direct air services to almost every major UK city, with BEA (or a subsidiary, like Northeast Airlines to Newcastle) operating most of them. I've used a few, including BEA's (and subsequently BA's) service from Heathrow to Jersey and British Midland Airways' Heathrow to Manchester and Heathrow to East Midlands service.

Despite the fact that the United Kingdom is where some of the earliest air services began, air travel within the UK has never really taken off. Even though the largest urban areas have well-established services to Heathrow, domestic flights have started, stopped, started again, and stopped again, and the arguments are not new.

By any yardstick, British Airways is one of the world's greatest airlines, as were the two state-owned carriers that formed it—BOAC and BEA. All three are synonymous with Heathrow. Although it was not the first carrier to fly from the airport, since the day Heathrow opened, Britain's national airline has been the airport's dominant carrier in the same way that Pan American were always New York's most visible presence, American Airlines at Dallas/Fort Worth, Air Canada at Montreal, Air France at Paris, or QANTAS at Sydney.

At its height, BEA had the largest European network of any of the continent's airlines, and BOAC had built an equally unrivalled intercontinental route system. The only other airline that could fly you right around the globe was Pan Am, and BOAC even had a mini-hub at JFK, the US carrier's home base, which is why BOAC and British Airways still have their own terminal at New York—the only non-US airline at JFK to do so. Only West Africa and South America, with the exception of Rio de Janeiro and Sao Paulo, did not feature on BOAC's route map. When the government decided to merge the two UK airlines, creating British Airways, the result was an airline that was huge by any standards, with a huge fleet, a huge army of staff and, significantly, huge losses. In this instance, two were probably better than one. Even so, while both airlines had lost money, at times they had also made large profits. Part of the problem was the habit of successive governments telling both airlines how to run their business and what aircraft to buy (like the VC10 and Trident instead of the Boeings that both carriers wanted) in order to protect jobs in the UK. It is a noble aim for any government, but not one that sits easily with what is in the best commercial interest of any business, including airlines.

After the Conservative party won the 1979 general election, in 1981 Sir John King, later to become Lord King, was appointed Chairman of British Airways. King's brief was relatively simple, although far from easy—he was to prepare the loss-making giant for privatisation. He appointed Colin Marshall as CEO in 1983, and between them, the two men transformed British Airways into one of the most efficient and profitable air carriers in the world. They did so at a time when many other airlines, and especially those that remained state-owned, were struggling. BA's fleet and route system were revamped and Landor Associates of California were brought in to design a new branding and advertising campaign. Over 23,000 jobs were shed in the early 1980s, though King managed to do so while boosting staff morale and modernising operations at the same time. By the time King and Marshall were done, British Airways probably merited the tag of 'The World's Favourite Airline'.

This is not to say that BA is immune from criticism. Sometimes it is deserved and sometimes not, but like any modern airline, BA must make money or fail, and it is at the mercy of factors sometimes beyond its control—the price of oil being one of the more obvious examples.

It was not always so. The business of carrying people, their possessions, and fee-paying cargo from one place to another (and especially between different countries) has until recently been the preserve of a government-chosen instrument. In the case of air travel, it was the government-sanctioned airline. However, this is not as simple as it might seem.

In order to run an airline service between two countries, the two governments had to agree what were known as 'Bilateral Air Travel Agreements'. For the most part, these treaties allowed each country to nominate one airline, or sometimes two, to fly services. The option to allow two airlines was mostly at the behest of the US, which, as a larger country with a substantially higher population, had more airlines. Since the UK was so much smaller (and, at that time, had just one national carrier), the agreement favoured the US. Governments will naturally almost always do what they consider to be best for their own people, but it made BOAC's globe-encircling achievements all the more noteworthy. Bilateral air treaties originated after the Second World War, and most countries had state-owned national airlines—BOAC, Air France, Sabena (Belgium), Alitalia (Italy), Japan Air Lines, Aeroflot (the former USSR), LOT (Poland), Iberia (Spain), and TAP (Portugal). There were some notable exceptions, such as Swissair (who went bankrupt and closed down, just as a number of other previously state-owned airlines have done) and the US carriers. Airlines in the United States were privately owned, but their business was tightly regulated both within the country and outside it, just as it was in Britain and almost everywhere. In the UK, however, with the establishment of BOAC and then BEA, there wasn't much room for anybody else. Nevertheless, in the 1940s there was an abundance of cheap aircraft—most of them no longer needed by the RAF—and an even greater abundance of people who believed they knew what to do with them, despite the obstacles.

Harold Bamberg was one such man, and his enthusiasm for aircraft stemmed from his former occupation as a wartime pilot. He formed Eagle Aviation Ltd on 14 April 1948. Eagle began operations by transporting fruit from Italy and Spain for merchants in Covent Garden. The first aircraft, a Handley Page Halifax converted bomber, was soon joined by a second. Both aircraft had seen extensive service (along with two others) during the Berlin Airlift, an event which, for a time at least, saved many of the UK's fledging airlines from going out of business.

Eagle did quite well, and by August 1951 the company had won the first government trooping contract awarded by the War Office; the Eagle aircraft were used to transport troops between the UK and Singapore. There was only so much that the RAF could do in transporting service personnel around the world; it was also cheaper to give a civilian airline the work instead of buying bigger fleets of passenger-carrying aircraft for the Air Force to use, not to mention increasing the size of RAF airfields to base them at. Eagle's trooping activities helped keep its fleet busy, and operations moved to a new base some way down the Great Southwest Road, also known as the A30. Further away from London, the road brings you to Blackbushe Airfield, which was referred to as London's second airport at the time.

Charter services were not restricted in the same way as regular scheduled services, and they were not seen as a threat to national airlines or their interests. BOAC and BEA had their hands full with operating their regular routes, and they showed little interest in carrying Her Majesty's Armed Services personnel around the world, leaving what they saw as the crumbs for the likes of the independent carriers like Eagle Aviation. In addition, steadily growing passenger charter operations included the first aerial cruises around the Mediterranean.

Bamberg was an ambitious man. In 1953, the company launched secondary scheduled services in association with BEA, from whom Eagle had purchased a large fleet of Vickers Vikings. Creating a new company, Eagle Airways, to operate the new services (leaving Eagle Aviation to run all non-scheduled operations, including trooping flights), the first service departed Blackbushe on 6 June 1953 to Belgrade via Munich. Aalborg and Gothenburg soon followed, as did domestic flights within the UK and further international routes to western European cities not served by the national carriers. In 1954, the UK Ministry of Aviation granted Eagle permission to operate a new type of low-fare service that combined air travel and overseas holiday accommodation, known as Inclusive Tour (IT) flights. For the population of a country still carrying the scars of war, the prospect of a cheap holiday was irresistible, and the concept enabled the airline to circumvent the restrictions that prevented private airlines from competing with their state-owned counterparts. Acquiring the Lunn travel agency chain, Eagle's first IT flights operated to destinations in Italy and Spain (including Majorca), and by 1955 all the company's aircraft carried the Eagle Airways operating name.

Always pushing his company toward the world stage, Bamberg then formed Eagle Airways (Bermuda) and in May 1958, launched regular service between Bermuda and New York, competing directly with three of the world's most powerful airlines—BOAC, Pan Am and Eastern Air Lines, the two US airlines on the route. BOAC were able to serve Bermuda from New York because the island was a British colony and BOAC was registered in Britain, but Eagle Airways (Bermuda) was a Bermuda-based company, so they could get around the treaty restrictions. Offering lower fares, additional routes quickly developed and traffic volumes on the Nassau to Miami and Bermuda to JFK routes grew to the point where a four-times-a-day service was offered on the former and a similar, three-times-daily operation ran on the latter. This increased Eagle's market share on the routes, in addition to the overall British market share. So successful were Eagle becoming that the airline launched services to London with all-economy-configured Douglas DC-6C aircraft. Bermuda's status as a British colony also meant that no reciprocal approvals from overseas authorities were needed and Eagle's new direct Bermuda to London flights were a cheaper and faster alternative to BOAC's DC-7C services, which were routed to New York first. By using Bermudan and therefore foreign-registered aircraft on the London service, Eagle were able to get around the restrictive licensing provisions (including those contained in the forthcoming Civil Aviation (Licensing) Act, 1960) as it only applied to UK aircraft.

One might well ask at this point, what does a thrusting upstart like Eagle and its ambitious owner have to do with the steadily developing home of BOAC and BEA west of London, sandwiched between the Bath Road and the Great South West Road?

In June 1958, Gatwick Airport reopened after a new runway and terminal had been built. The Sussex airfield was now designated as London's second airport as Blackbushe was considered unsuitable, not capable of further expansion, too far from London, and difficult to access by road. Gatwick was on the main rail line from London to Brighton; the airport had its own mainline railway station from the day its original terminal opened in 1936, a facility included in the 1958 terminal. The station remains within the airport's terminal to this day, and it is very busy. The airport also had better road links, so Blackbushe closed to commercial air traffic in 1960 and Bamberg moved his airline to a new base—Heathrow.

Eagle, along with Gatwick-based British United Airways (BUA)—its primary independent competitor, led by Managing Director Freddie Laker—had campaigned ceaselessly to bring about a change in legislation that had given their state-owned counterparts a virtual monopoly on scheduled services and the result was the Civil Aviation (Licensing) Act of 1960. The act abolished BOAC and BEA's rights to run both international and domestic flights and, theoretically at least, allowed the independents equal opportunities to develop such routes. All airlines, including BOAC and BEA, would now have to apply for route licenses and be able to object to other airlines getting them. Eagle agreed with British United Airlines and Caledonian Airways, another independent airline, that regular scheduled operations were the only viable way to build an airline with a long-term future. The independents had successfully argued that the existing nature of their business—mainly trooping, *ad hoc* charters, and IT flying—made forward planning difficult because of extreme seasonality and generally low margins. Eagle saw its future primarily as an international scheduled passenger and freight carrier with transatlantic ambitions. With another UK airline suddenly established in their backyard, both BOAC and BEA began to take notice, and even more so when the Cunard Line acquired a controlling stake in Eagle in March 1960. Renamed as 'Cunard Eagle', the airline was now forming a substantial operation at Heathrow, ordering two brand-new Boeing 707 long-haul jets (both powered by the same Rolls-Royce engines that BOAC's 707s used). When the newly constituted Air Transport Licensing Board (ATLB) awarded the company a licence to operate a scheduled service on the prime Heathrow to New York JFK sector, it gave the UK two airlines on the route and created parity with Pan Am and TWA.

BOAC were, to put it mildly, a bit peeved. As the national airline, and one that knew its market well, BOAC felt that it alone was in a position to operate long-haul services from Heathrow. The company mounted an appeal against the ATLB's decision to the then-aviation minister Peter Thorneycroft, who had the authority to either accept or reject the decisions of the ATLB. BOAC's appeal was successful; the company used its order for forty-five British-built Standard and Super VC10 jets and an earlier ministerial promise not to permit another British competitor on the route as leverage. Cunard Eagle's licence was revoked in November 1961.

BOAC then mounted something of a coup by forming BOAC-Cunard as a new joint venture with Cunard. The state-owned carrier provided 70 per cent of the capital for the new company and eight of its Boeing 707-436 jets. Eagle's long-haul operations—including the two new 707s—were merged into BOAC-Cunard before delivery of the second 707 in June 1962. Although Harold Bamberg was appointed to the board of BOAC-Cunard, he resigned in 1963 and reconstituted Eagle by buying back control from Cunard. The airline's official name changed to 'British Eagle International Airlines Ltd'.

As the 1960s progressed, British Eagle began operating domestic services from Heathrow to Glasgow, Edinburgh, Belfast, and Liverpool, in direct competition with BEA. Although still operating long-haul charters, Eagle suffered heavy losses in the UK and suspended the services in February 1965.

BUA then applied to the ATLB to have the licences transferred to them since Eagle weren't operating the flights. The 'use them or lose them' argument has been applied countless times since in various airline wars—sometimes successfully, sometimes not. BUA wanted to operate the routes with new BAC111 jets from its Gatwick base, pointing out that its services would primarily be intended as domestic feeders for its growing international scheduled operations—having carved out something of a niche long-haul network from Gatwick, especially to West Africa. BUA claimed that this was supported by government policy giving preference to Gatwick's development to improve its use, thus enabling it to become profitable, and that it would relieve congestion at Heathrow. BUA also argued that the use of a different London terminal serving a different market would divert little traffic from BEA, minimising the competitive impact on the state-owned airline. In addition to British Eagle's licenses, BUA also sought scheduled service licences for London–Birmingham and London–Manchester, also to be flown from Gatwick.

Eagle were given little choice but to restart services and operations between Heathrow and Glasgow began on 5 July 1965, at a frequency of three return flights per day. Two of these flew non-stop while the remaining one went via Liverpool. Having learned the lessons from their earlier attempt, net profits recovered to £350,000 on the routes and Bamberg announced an order for three BAC111-300s, including a further three options, marking Eagle's comeback as a jet operator. By 1966, BEA were operating Comet 4Bs and both BUA and Eagle had the BAC111 in service between London and Scotland.

In 1967, British Eagle, BUA, Caledonian, and Transglobe, another UK independent, all applied to the ATLB for licences to operate scheduled and non-scheduled services directly in competition with BOAC on a number of long-haul routes. In the ATLB hearings frenzy, the independent airlines objected to each other and BOAC objected to everybody. The independent airline applications were turned down on the basis that none were financially strong enough to make the routes profitable. BOAC, however, were.

After twenty years of flying, by 14 April 1968, British Eagle were in the top five of British airlines, behind BEA, BOAC, and BUA, but ahead of Caledonian. However, later that same year, BOAC made a complaint to the ATLB that Eagle were misusing the terms and conditions of its inclusive tour licence by promoting services as if they were scheduled services. The ATLB found in BOAC's favour.

British Eagle and its sister companies ceased trading at midnight on 6 November 1968 and went into voluntary liquidation two days later. The airline's last aircraft movement was an arrival from Rotterdam at Heathrow the following day. As well as the loss of the company's Caribbean licence, the end of the trooping contracts, along with other charters and economic difficulties, had made British Eagle an increasingly unviable business.

British summers can sometimes be glorious in their warmth, but they mostly tend to be slightly disappointing. The lure of sun and sandy beaches had led to numerous airlines going into the inclusive-tour business, Eagle being one and BUA and Caledonian being two more. Another was Autair. All faced a similar problem; in the winter, the fleets of aircraft needed for busy summers flying British holidaymakers to Spain were sitting around, not doing very much, and thus costing the airlines money instead of earning it. Some leased their spare aircraft to other airlines during the off-peak seasons, but most believed (as Eagle, BUA and Caledonian had already suggested) that only year-round scheduled services would bring them sufficient profits. With Eagle's wings permanently clipped, Autair moved in.

Formed at Luton Airport in 1957 and originally named Argus Air Transport, on 27 September 1963 the name changed to 'Autair International Airways'. By spring 1969, five BAC 111-400s operated Autair's IT flights, primarily under contract to Clarkson's Tours. These carried most of the airline's 500,000 annual charter passengers, which far outnumbered the 66,000 using its scheduled services each year.

From 1 April 1969, the airline's scheduled operation in London centred at Heathrow's Terminal 1, joining Teesside services, which had already moved to Heathrow from the company's Luton base on 1 November 1967.

The then-deputy chairman of Autair International, Mr G. H. G. Threlfall, gave a lecture to the Air Transport Group of the Royal Aeronautical Society. His comments were reported in the 3 April 1969 edition of *Flight International* magazine:

'In order to study the future of domestic air services, it is necessary to look at the past, and draw certain lessons from it. In doing this, one is struck by the amazing and almost unparalleled history of failures that there had been. It occurs to me,' he continued, 'That if airlines were forced to study the history of UK air services over the last 50 years, they might then be slightly less keen on developing new domestic services themselves.'

Tracing the development of domestic services in Britain, Threlfall noted that there had been little activity up to 1932 and that Imperial Airways had not shown much interest in European, let alone domestic routes. From 1932, growth speeded up and by 1934 the route coverage of the country was surprisingly comprehensive. In 1935 there were 19 airlines operating 76 routes, although Threlfall doubted if any of them were really profitable.

In 1936 the Maybury Committee had been set up to consider 'the development of civil aviation in the United Kingdom.' When they reported in January 1937, their two main recommendations were, first that a route licensing system should be established to regulate the situation and to ensure that the existing cut-throat competition was eliminated, and secondly that Government assistance was essential.

'I would also like to quote one other very important aspect of their report,' Threlfall said, 'Which read: "It would be wrong to discuss air transport and surface transport in terms of pure competition; the true approach, if both are to benefit, and if the community is to gain the greatest advantage from the potentialities of the air, is to regard them as complimentary."'

In January 1939, the Government had implemented the Maybury proposals. Nearly 50 routes were licensed, and by the outbreak of war on September 3 nearly 50,000 passengers had been carried and £70,000 in subsidy had been paid at a rate of 6*d* per capacity ton-mile. After the war many routes had been restarted but when BEA took over, a number of these were closed down again—including London-Manchester and London-Liverpool.

'The most remarkable aspect of this disorganised post-war period [1945–1960],' said Mr. Threlfall, 'was the fantastic number of airlines that tried to run domestic scheduled services, and then went broke. It was bad enough before the war with nearly 20 airlines unsuccessfully trying to make a go of it, but from 1945 to 1969 I have counted the incredible number of 58 private airlines that tried to run UK domestic scheduled services, and 45 that did operate them, of which only two are still going under the same ownership. Of the remaining 56 unfortunate airlines, I calculate that nine are still operating because they have been taken over by someone else and the other 47 have disappeared.'

Threllfall's remarks were prophetic indeed. In the summer of 1969, just months after his lecture, Autair announced its decision to withdraw all scheduled services 'irrevocably' following an unsuccessful request for government subsidies. Both BEA and BOAC received them, but both were state-owned.

By that time, Autair's scheduled network from Heathrow served Belfast, Blackpool, Carlisle, the Channel Islands, Dundee, Glasgow, Hull, the Isle of Man and Teesside in the UK, along with Amsterdam and Dublin. Scheduled services accounted for 12 per cent of Autair's turnover and were estimated to have generated an annual loss of £150,000, with only London-Teesside said to be profitable. On 31 October 1969, Autair's scheduled services ended, and with BUA and Caledonian still based at Gatwick, it left Heathrow to BOAC and BEA.

Threllfall's lecture may have been made early in 1969, but the remarks are still valid forty-seven years later. The British Isles are quite small, and until relatively recently they have not been especially heavily populated compared to larger countries. Unless there is a substantial body of water between two places (and with water choppy enough to make boat crossings uncomfortable), there are a few places around the UK that are not close enough to make surface travel more practical than flight, particularly when considering one has to get to and from the airport at each end of their journey. London to Belfast will involve one such boat ride, as will journeys to the Channel Islands or the Isle of Man. London to Birmingham, on the other hand, is a mere hop at a little more than an hour and a half by train. Air links once existed between the two, but this was when trains were much slower.

The country is also full of hills, mountains, valleys, and undulating land. Not too much of the landscape is flat; rail lines thus tend to wind a little as they rise and fall through the countryside, which doesn't do much to help speed the train from city to city. Even so, Britain is where the train was invented, so it has a well-established tradition of rail travel. In comparison, flying is a much newer way of getting around, and the British largely tend to be sticklers for tradition.

Until the advent of deregulation and low-cost airlines, air travel was also the preserve of the wealthy, who represented a small percentage of the population. Train fares were much cheaper, hence Threlfall's comment about government subsidies in his lecture. Many of those air services also commented on were not from London, but between regional cities; before the war, smaller aircraft were used, operating from grass runways. By the end of the Second World War, many airfields had acquired concrete runways that were laid as a result of the hostilities. They were not especially long runways, although still suitable for smaller aircraft but not the larger ones that came along within ten years of the war ending. This is one reason why BEA dropped so many domestic routes and BEA's primary reason for being was to link Britain with Europe.

Domestic services were never a priority unless it was to connect places like Glasgow and Edinburgh to London and then on to Europe; this was before aircraft had the range to fly from Scotland, Northern Ireland, and the north of England non-stop. Even so, BEA did have a reasonably comprehensive network—not only from Heathrow, but also between other cities in the UK, branded as 'BEA Inter-Britain'. Much of the network remained until the airline stopped being state-owned and subsidies thus ended. Once the company had been merged with BOAC to form British Airways, then privatised and had to stand on its own two feet, it was another matter. The only reason for operating any domestic service was to link with long-haul routes at Heathrow, and as Heathrow got increasingly busy, the amount of runway time dramatically decreased; with aircraft now having the range to go from regional British cities to European destinations non-stop (and, in some cases, even further), the need to go via Heathrow became less pressing. UK domestic services no longer made enough money to survive, as British Eagle, Autair, and, later, British Caledonian found out.

British Caledonian, or BCAL as they were often known, were based at Gatwick, not Heathrow, and came into existence through a merger between British United and Caledonian Airways. The intention was to become Britain's 'second-force' airline and to provide competition to BA. At its height, the airline operated domestic services from Gatwick to all the major UK cities and a number of European routes. They also grew by running long-haul services from Gatwick to places not served by BA from Heathrow; after all, competition only goes so far. When they did begin to serve cities that British Airways also served—such as New York—things began to unravel. Although BA were criticised at the time, British Caledonian were a week away from going bust when BA bought them in 1988.

Gatwick's problem is that it has never had the necessary amount or variety of services that Heathrow has had. It also has one runway. Airlines like Air UK, British Caledonian, British Eagle, British Island Airways, British Midland, and Dan Air have come and gone, along with many more. All operated both domestic and international scheduled services, but none had the economies of scale that both British Airways and Heathrow has. All failed. The latest to try was Virgin Atlantic, with their 'Little Red' brand stepping into the void created by British Airway's takeover of British Midland. British Midland had themselves stepped into the shoes of British Caledonian when they were taken over by BA; for a time, they successfully built a network of services from Heathrow, in direct competition with British Airways. BA's tendency to acquire their competitors (they also took over Dan Air) has been criticised by many, but in fairness, had they not, those airlines would have gone bankrupt anyway. Having started operations in March 2013, Little Red ceased flying at the end of September 2015 because they simply could not make enough money from their services to and from Manchester, Edinburgh, and Aberdeen feeding sufficient numbers of passengers onto Virgin's long-haul routes at Heathrow.

The presence of big international carriers like Emirates (Dubai), United (US), and a host of others at places like Manchester, and the multitude of direct flights from other airports around the UK to European cities, does suggest that the population is high enough to support them, or they wouldn't be operated. Airlines are very quick to drop services that don't make money, and the mass of flights to Amsterdam from around the UK means KLM do very nicely out of connecting passengers that originate from the UK to the rest of the world. Paris can be held in the same bracket; Air France are the other half of the joint Air France/KLM Group.

Amsterdam Schiphol connects to twenty-seven destinations in the UK, while Paris Charles de Gaulle has sixteen UK routes. In 2016, domestic flights to other UK cities from Heathrow are limited to Glasgow, Edinburgh, Leeds/Bradford, Manchester, Newcastle, and Belfast City, and all are flown by British Airways, with only Aer Lingus competing between London and Belfast. This gives a total of just six domestic routes. But if one looks, it is easy to see why domestic services have not worked out at Heathrow.

Amsterdam has six runways and a terminal complex much bigger than Heathrow, even with the latter's new terminals. Paris Charles de Gaulle (CDG) has four runways, and little Heathrow, with its mere two runways, would fit inside the perimeters of both European airports with room to spare. The Netherlands is an even smaller country, geographically speaking, than the UK, and it is even more densely populated, but it has never had a viable domestic route network. However, the Dutch have a long-standing aviation tradition, and decades ago they recognised that air travel was key to the country's prosperity. Schiphol Airport and KLM represent a drive to capture and retain this business. France, another country with aviation history, has done the same thing with CDG. Heathrow has never had the runway infrastructure to support a viable domestic network, with neither the runway nor terminal capacity that is available at AMS and CDG—and yet neither of the European airports are as busy as Heathrow.

On 23 March 2015, well before the Runway Commission made its deliberations public, *The Telegraph* reported:

> Heathrow has pledged to create more flights to regional airports in the UK if it wins its hotly-contested bid for expansion and has set aside £10m for the development of new domestic routes.
>
> The West London airport said the multi-million pound conditional commitment would be able to fund five new local flight paths for three years, in addition to the four extra routes that easyJet has announced it would look to operate if a Heathrow expansion is confirmed.
>
> Heathrow, which is currently operating at full capacity, has suggested its new routes could include Newquay, Humberside and Liverpool, while easyJet has said it would look to fly to Inverness, Belfast International, the Isle of Man and Jersey.
>
> Saad Hammad, chief executive of Flybe—the UK's largest regional airline, which does not currently serve any routes connecting to Heathrow—said that he 'welcomes the commitment of Heathrow to enhance regional connectivity both within current runway capacity constraints and in the event of new runway development.' Commending Heathrow for 'taking practical steps to be more inclusive,' Mr Hammad added: 'Our national hub in the South East must address the needs of all the nations and regions of the UK not just those living within the boundary of the M25.'

Interesting developments—especially EasyJet's potential appearance at Heathrow.

Heathrow's runway capacity does still have enough room—just—for the existing flights to Glasgow and Edinburgh, as well as services to Manchester, Newcastle, Leeds/Bradford, and British Airways' and Aer Lingus' Belfast City services. All of these destinations are far enough away to make it worthwhile to fly. However, on Wednesday 1 July 2015, the day of the Runway Commission's announcement, *The Herald* reported:

SCOTLAND could end up with even fewer connections to an expanded Heathrow than it has now unless the government reforms how it uses public subsidies to support domestic routes, the Airports Commission has warned. In its long-awaited report, the Commission said adding a third runway to the UK hub offered the 'strongest case' for boosting regional and international connectivity, but cautioned that growing demand for landing slots meant that 'even an expanded Heathrow may accommodate fewer domestic routes in future'.

The number of services between Scotland and Heathrow has tumbled from 50 to 35 in the last decade. Inverness has had no daily connections with the hub since 1997 while flights to Heathrow from Glasgow and Edinburgh have been cut by a third in the last 20 years.

Scottish business leaders have been vocal in their support for a third runway at Heathrow over the alternatives of a second runway at Gatwick or extending Heathrow's Northern runway.

Heathrow bosses have vowed to protect and increase regional services by creating a £10 million start-up fund to support establishment of new routes, and want to cut landing charges by £10 per passenger on UK routes from January 2016.

In its report, the Airports Commission said that by 2040, domestic services could utilise "136-175 additional daily slot pairs" at an expanded Heathrow compared to 55 currently.

But it noted that 'a number of competing pressures may limit the increase in domestic services to an enlarged Heathrow'.

It stated: 'One such pressure could be continuing competition from overseas hubs, which may still be able to offer cheaper services, higher frequencies, or more convenient connections on some routes.

'An expanded Heathrow is also likely to see rapid growth in demand, which may relatively quickly begin to exert pressure on slots during the most popular periods.

'The Commission's forecasts reflect these pressures and suggest that without specific measures to support domestic connectivity even an expanded Heathrow may accommodate fewer domestic routes in future than the seven served currently.' [Including the now-discontinued Little Red service to Aberdeen.]

The report stressed that there was 'no viable legal basis' under EU competition rules to guarantee a fixed number of slots to domestic services, but urged the government 'reinterpret' Public Service Obligations [PSO] so that they could be deployed 'more widely than at present'.

PSOs allow the state to subsidise carriers on routes which are not commercially viable.

However, the Commission suggested that since access to an expanded Heathrow—in particular up to 12 new long-haul destinations—was vital to the 'economic and social development' of the UK as a whole and should therefore 'be seen as an important factor when considering the establishment of PSOs'.

Emma Gilthorpe, Heathrow's Strategy, Planning & Regulation Director, said the third runway would pave the way to new connections and increased frequency to emerging markets in South America, the Far East and China, and it was 'absolutely critical' to link Scotland to these consumers.

'Our proposal for a landing charge discount will make that more viable and it was part of the rationale for why we put that forward because we were keen to regain those critical routes.'

Liz Cameron, Director and Chief Executive of Scottish Chambers of Commerce, said: 'The expansion of capacity at Heathrow has many potential benefits for Scotland, but only if our air links to Heathrow improve'....

The Commission's recommendation will pose a headache for Government, however, with a number of senior Conservatives including London Mayor Boris Johnson and Zac Goldsmith, opposed.

Willie Walsh, chief executive of British Airways owner IAG, has previously said that a third runway was a 'lost cause' that no Government would have the bottle to carry out.

The Commission conceded that the alternative plans were also 'feasible', leaving the door open to Ministers to reach their own conclusion.

A second runway at Gatwick would also boost capacity but 'would be more focused on short-haul intra-European routes and the economic benefits considerably smaller', said the Commission.

A new runway, expected to cost £17.6 billion to deliver, will boost GDP by up to £147 billion over 60 years and create more than 70,000 new jobs by 2050, the report concluded.

Sir Howard Davies, the chair of the Commission, said: 'Heathrow is best-placed to provide the type of capacity which is most urgently required: long haul destinations to new markets. It provides the greatest benefits for business passengers, freight operators and the broader economy.'

Patrick McLoughlin, Secretary of State for Transport, said he would report back to Parliament in the autumn to reveal the Government's plans.

He said: 'This is a vital moment for the future of our aviation industry. All those with an interest in this important question are expecting us to act decisively.'

On the one hand, one of the reasons put forward to build a third runway is to expand long-haul flights to new markets; on the other, doing so may reduce the potential for Heathrow to see a return of domestic services. At the end of July, Boris Johnson's office released the following statement:

Nearly half the flights between Heathrow and the rest of the UK are set for the scrapheap if a third runway is given the green light according to data published by the Airports Commission. Today (31 July) the Mayor of London wrote to the leaders of cities and regions around Great Britain to warn them of the situation. He also alerted the government that it will need to be in a position to explain which of the UK cities currently served by Heathrow would be expected to retain a link to the airport were a third runway to be approved.

Over the last twenty-five years connections between Heathrow and other UK destinations have dwindled from 18 to just seven. And it is widely agreed that one of the main aims of increasing aviation capacity in the UK should be to provide regional airports with improved access to the country's hub airport and its links to long haul destinations.

But buried deep within the final report published by the Airports Commission earlier this month is the astonishing forecast that a three-runway Heathrow would see regional links decline further and the airport would only offer routes to four UK destinations.

The Mayor of London, Boris Johnson, said: 'The final decision on where to provide new aviation capacity needs to be in the interest of the entire country and this astonishing admission makes clear that a third runway at Heathrow would fail that test on every count. The hoax that it would be of benefit to our regions has been thoroughly exposed, and it is now clear that even the existing UK links to and from Heathrow are under threat. The only long term solution to Britain's aviation needs is a hub airport with the potential for multiple runways and the spare capacity to allow domestic routes to flourish. It is what our global rivals are doing, it is the right thing to do, and it is what must happen here.'

Domestic links to Heathrow have been squeezed out over several decades in favour of more lucrative long haul services and the Airports Commission's forecast is that a three-runway Heathrow will fail to stem that decline. The only glimmer of hope they offer other regions around the UK is that domestic connections might be saved from the axe through the use of taxpayer-funded Public Service Obligations. But today the Mayor's team highlighted serious questions around the practicality of doing so.

In the Mayor's letter he also said that, when the government issues its final judgement on a third runway at Heathrow, it must be in a position to be able to answer questions such as:

Which of the UK airports currently served by Heathrow would be expected to retain one of the four routes forecast by the Airports Commission to be available?

What Public Service Obligations arrangements would it attempt to put in place, for how long and at what cost to protect existing routes under threat of closure?

What Public Service Obligations arrangements would it attempt to put in place, for how long and at what cost to ensure that UK domestic connectivity to Heathrow and beyond can flourish by enabling additional UK cities to be served?

The Mayor of London's chief adviser on aviation, Daniel Moylan, said: 'Any attempt to impose a state sponsored domestic route network would clearly face the risk of legal challenges. And would the taxpayer be willing to pay for it? Public Service Obligations are designed for 'peripheral and development regions' so there will be questions of illegal state aid if the government follows the Airports Commission's guidance on this. It would involve taking a huge and unpopular gamble with taxpayers' money.'

All this represents a confusing set of contradictions. Domestic services have been lost to Heathrow because of runway capacity. If smaller aircraft were used to handle the indisputably lower number of passengers that would fly domestic routes, connecting Heathrow to more UK airports, this would result in more aircraft movements, and more aircraft movements require a larger runway capacity. It therefore seems logical to suggest that if a three-runway Heathrow would still be unable to support reinstated domestic services; the airport needs to increase its capacity to more than three runways, just as Amsterdam, Paris, and (more recently) Frankfurt have done.

Today there are eleven major airlines operating within the UK—Aurigny Air Services and Blue Islands (both operating flights to, from, and within the Channel Islands), BMI Regional, British Airways, Citywing, Eastern Airways, EasyJet, Flybe, Jet2.com, Monarch Airlines, and Scottish-based Logan Air. Only one of them operates into Heathrow.

Fly to Glasgow and connect with a flight to Barra Airport, on the Outer Hebrides, and you'll arrive at the only airport in the world where all the flights use a beach as a runway. Services are subject to the tide being out—but at least there are no contradictory discussions over how many beaches to have.

18

BAA Equals HAL

I did not fully understand the dreaded term 'terminal illness' until I saw Heathrow for myself.

Dennis Potter

Heathrow Airport Limited (HAL) started life as The British Airports Authority. When Peter Masefield became its first chairman, the newly created BAA took over the ownership and operation of Heathrow, along with Gatwick, Stansted, and Glasgow Prestwick, later expanding to include the airports of Glasgow Abbotsinch (which replaced the city's earlier airport at Renfrew), Edinburgh, and Aberdeen. This gave the BAA seven airports to look after. As a state-owned organisation, it was responsible directly to the British government and the policies pursued by whichever political party ran the country at the time. Since 1945, only two parties have held a majority in the British government—the Conservatives and the Labour Party.

Labour have always favoured nationalisation and state ownership, while the Conservatives usually preferred private ownership. However, even they tacitly accepted that the state would own and operate much of Britain's infrastructure, such as the national gas and electricity companies, British Rail, BEA, BOAC, and subsequently (and for a time, at least) British Airways and the BAA. State ownership can bring some benefits—principally, that any profit goes straight into the national coffers. Accountability is another benefit. However, state ownership also brings responsibilities, and one of those is to ensure that whatever the enterprise, it must receive regular investment to keep its operations current and efficient. It is here that state ownership tends to fall down a little. When taxpayers are the ones footing the bill, they are sometimes inclined to ask where their money goes, so some governments prefer to avoid spending it altogether—unless it's on something that looks good in newspaper headlines, or a pet project dear to the party's membership.

The other big problem with state ownership is that when the government changes hands, the policies of the incumbent and previous parties can conflict with each other, resulting in public enterprises being pulled one way and then another at the whim of the current government. Publicly owned industries are also sometimes ordered to buy British-made supplies, as was the case when BEA were ordered to buy the Trident and

BOAC were ordered to buy the VC10. In this respect, the enterprises are unable to make decisions based on purely commercial grounds, so they are at risk of losing a lot of money.

The British Airports Authority, however, did make money—especially at Heathrow, although its profits were somewhat diluted as the Authority was obliged to spend money on other airports in the group. The BAA also looked after enthusiasts, maintaining the roof gardens on top of the Queen's Building and T2. However, things began to change in the 1980s. Profitable or not, it costs a huge amount of money to redesign and redevelop airports, and a state-owned business can get the money needed from only two sources— its profits (if it has them) or the government.

The majority of the government's money comes from taxpayers, and, as previously mentioned, taxpayers tend to get a little prickly when large amounts of the money they have to hand over is spent on what could be seen as vanity projects—like big new airport terminals or railway lines. The current UK government is frequently criticised for its decision to spend billions on a new high-speed rail line (HS2) from London to the Midlands and the north of England (including a link to Heathrow, although not Scotland). Already underway is CrossRail, a new underground mainline rail track linking Heathrow and HS1, which runs into London from the Kent coast and the Channel ports. HS1 was built as part of the Channel Tunnel Rail Link and went ahead without a murmur of protest from anybody. It does have logic—HS1 to CrossRail and HS2. It is the kind of joined-up planning that has been missing for decades. The government's problem is that it is cutting its expenditure in many other areas—areas that are seen as more vital than HS2. The new line, HS2, will not be built for another twenty years.

When Margaret Thatcher's Conservative Party won the general election in 1979, ministers knew that taxpayers would be unable to provide the huge amount of money needed to renew and modernise Heathrow, the rail network, and water, gas, and electricity suppliers. Most of the country's state-owned businesses were losing huge amounts of money each year—including British Airways, which had been formed out of the merger of BOAC and BEA only a few years earlier. Only privately-owned businesses can raise money from outside sources, like a stock market floatation. The government's response was to privatise pretty much everything, which some saw as a good move and others saw as selling off the family silver. The Airports Act 1986 mandated the creation of BAA Plc as a vehicle by which stock market funds could be raised. Each of the seven BAA airports was made into a separate company, each wholly owned by BAA Plc. British Airways was successfully privatised in February 1987, with BAA Plc also passing into private ownership in July of the same year.

The full name of the British Airports Authority was then changed, with 'Authority' being dropped. For the sake of brand recognition, the company became simply 'BAA', with the initials not actually standing for anything—despite much of the public and the media continuing to refer to it by its former title. Outwardly, little had changed, but for enthusiasts, the roof gardens began to get smaller and smaller, with the portion on top of the Queen's Building closed off completely. This left a small central section on the roof of T2 itself.

My father had a love affair with Paris. He would go for a quick weekend in the French capital at the drop of a hat, and in 1989 I thought it would be nice to go and meet him when he flew back into Heathrow. Since he was flying with Air France, he was using T2, so I figured I stood a reasonable chance of getting some decent photographs—including the aircraft he would be on. I duly arrived at the remains of the roof gardens and went to the pay booth; it never cost much to use the viewing area, but they did have a closing time. My dad's flight was due to come in half an hour before closing, and I was there an hour before his flight was timed to arrive. The BAA-uniformed man in the booth was closing up, so I tapped on the window and pointed politely to the sign; he merely gave me a scowling look of disdain and pulled the blinds down. Such had become the attitude of BAA Plc. I also saw some disappointed families with young children being turned away at the same time.

A statement released during this period claimed: 'Heathrow Airport welcomes aircraft enthusiasts and spotters, provided they keep to the area reserved for them', meaning the roof gardens. This is not much use on a sunny summer afternoon, when surly and plain-rude pay-booth attendants want to slope off early. Plan B was the uppermost level of the car park next to T2, which gave a good view of runway 27 left/09 right at the time, in addition to the parking areas at the southern ends of T2 and T3. I got my photograph of Dad's Airbus A300 as it landed, for a change, on the cross-wind runway, No. 2. As shown it the layout's original plans from the 1940s, this was the third runway that Heathrow had always had—one that everybody now conveniently forgets about. The roof gardens would have presented a better view, but high barriers were subsequently put up on the car park's upper floors, closing off the airfield view from there too.

After becoming a private company, BAA's primary responsibility was to its shareholders, and thus it had a greater obligation to make money. Spotters and enthusiasts do not bring in sufficiently significant amounts to make it worthwhile to spend money on facilities for them. In order to make it a worthwhile venture, the fee for the public would have to be too high for most visitors to stomach. Still, the airport could benefit by taking a long-term view and charging a lower fee. However, shareholders tend to want to see the fastest-possible return on their investment. A publicly owned entity such as the old BAA has something of an obligation to the public (as does your local town council or city authority). The British Airports Authority was unstinting in its efforts to relate to and help the public. When I was at school, I did a class project on world airports; I wrote to the airport, telling them what I wanted and what for. They sent me stacks of information, as did other airports from around the world. I still have a bundle of public relations information given to me by the BAA between 1978 and 1980. Today, as a journalist, I receive information, press releases, and more (particularly if for a magazine article) from many airports around the world, including regular news releases from HAL.

HAL probably receive hundreds of enquiries a week, most of which they can't help with, and given the circumstances surrounding a new runway, they will be fielding a lot of uncomplimentary enquiries and comments as well, which doesn't help anybody. They also have to handle the media frenzy that can result after incidents like the one involving the protestors who staged the sit-in on runway 27 right's threshold. There will almost certainly be more of them.

As a company, HAL does a good job overall of running Heathrow. To run a major piece of infrastructure like the airport requires skill, talent, and expertise, and HAL have those in abundance. While no one can ever be immune to occasionally justified criticism, the new terminals and the billions spent on the airport are a testimony to HAL's stewardship, recognised by the airport's 'Best Airport in Europe' Airports Council International Europe (ACI Europe) award at the end of June 2015 (in the category of airports with more than 25 million passengers per year). Heathrow also won the ACI Europe 'Eco-Innovation Award' for efforts in energy efficiency, aviation noise research, and forward planning on the environment. HAL's aim of presenting London with a world-class and modern international gateway is impressive and realistic—and it does need the extra runways I referred to.

Heathrow Airport Holdings Limited, to give it its full title, today owns and operates only Heathrow, hence the name. The other airports that the group were responsible for were sold to other private interests as a result of a UK Competition Commission inquiry running from August 2008 to March 2009. The Commission announced that BAA, as it was at the time, would have to sell three of the seven UK airports it then owned—Gatwick, Stansted, and either Glasgow or Edinburgh. It was also confirmed that BAA would be compelled to sell them to privately-owned and independent companies within two years. The Commission's concerns were that the monopoly position held by BAA over London and the two Scottish airports could have 'adverse effects for both passengers and airlines'.

Gatwick was sold by October 2009 and the remaining airports were sold by the end of 2014, leaving the company to concentrate solely on Heathrow.

The Competition Commission's deliberations and decisions seem a little odd when one considers that Spanish company AENA owns and operates no less than fourteen major airports around the country, including Madrid. In France, both Paris airports—Orly and Charles de Gaulle—are owned by Aeroports de Paris. Stranger still, in the UK, Stansted (still perhaps unfairly seen as something of a poor relation in the hierarchy of London's airports) is now owned by the Manchester Airports Group (MAG), who also own Manchester, Bournemouth (where London-bound passengers arrived before Heathrow was opened), and East Midlands (which serves Nottingham, Derby, and Leicester). MAG is the largest UK-owned airport operator, serving around 42 million passengers every year. Remarkably, the group is not in private hands. According to its website, MAG is owned by:

Australian fund manager IFM Investors—35.5 per cent
Manchester City Council—35.5 per cent
The other nine Greater Manchester Councils—29 per cent as follows:
The Borough Council of Bolton
The Borough Council of Bury
The Oldham Borough Council
The Rochdale Borough Council
The Council of the City of Salford
The Metropolitan Borough Council of Stockport
The Tameside Metropolitan Borough Council

The Trafford Borough Council
The Wigan Borough Council.

The north-west city's airport was opened in 1938 by the local council and has remained in public ownership ever since. Although it grew steadily over the years, it is only during the past decade that it has grown to become the third-busiest airport in the UK, marginally busier than Stansted but behind the two primary London airports—and they do look after aviation enthusiasts.

The four London Airports, on the other hand, are owned by four separate companies, including MAG, which seems to do little to help joined-up thinking, planning, and service to the customers—both airlines and passengers. There is no 'London Airport System', a system originally envisaged as long ago as the 1940s, when Harold Balfour began his admittedly underhand machinations to get Heathrow built. The system was suggested again by the Millbourn Committee in 1957, and it was what Peter Masefield took on when he became Chairman of the BAA in April 1966—the result of the 1961 House of Commons Select Committee report that gave birth to BAA itself.

HAL is owned by a consortium headed by Spanish company Ferrovial, who specialise in transport and services infrastructure. HAL's head office is at the airport itself, in the Compass Centre on the northern perimeter of the airport. It earns its income from the fees levied on airlines and other operations within Heathrow, such as terminal retail rentals and property leased on its land, along with ownership and operation of the Heathrow Express train service.

19

Over and Out

When once you have tasted flight, you will forever walk the earth with your eyes turned skyward, for there you have been, and there you will always long to return.

Leonardo Da Vinci

Terminal 1, 1989—check-in for a British Midland Airways flight to Amsterdam. The aircraft is a Douglas DC9-30, which, gratifyingly, is parked at the first gate on T1's international pier, so there is a short walk to board. Parked next to a British Airways Lockheed L1011 TriStar 200, the DC9 is tiny. The even-smaller figures of the ground crew scurry about, loading and unloading. Pushback is on time, and a relatively short taxi takes the aircraft to the threshold of runway 27 right, along part of the taxiway that runs parallel to the crosswind third runway—the same third runway that everybody will have forgotten about (or just ignored) twenty-seven years after this flight.

My window seat on the left side of the aircraft reveals a brief sideways look at runway 27 right, stretching 3,902 metres into the distance, as we reach the holding point. Not visible, on the opposite side of the DC9, is the British Airways maintenance base, its huge hangars still dominating the airport's eastern end. A QANTAS Boeing 747-338 is cleared to depart ahead of our twin jet and it rumbles away into the misty morning, so our little Douglas is cleared to enter the runway onto the piano keys, the pilot turning left to align the DC9 to start its take-off run straight down the centre of the runway. Then we wait to let the disturbed air caused by the size of the 747's acceleration to subside; all large aircraft leave what is known as wake turbulence behind them, both on the runway itself and in the air after lifting off, and the amount of it can cause smaller aircraft to become uncontrollable. We wait a few moments before the engines throttle up, and then we are away. We go past Terminal 1, on the left, while on the right, unseen, are the remains of the original ramp on which BSAA's Lancastrian Starlight parked on the airport's first day of operations in 1946. The tents are now long gone, as are the more solid but still temporary buildings that replaced them. We go past Roy's cannon and Caesar's camp, lifting smoothly away from the runway and into the air just by the tunnel to the Central Terminal Area.

The left-hand window seat then gives the classic view of Terminal 3 and the 747-100s, -200s, and -300s of just a few of the world's airlines parked around the piers—four of

A Qantas Boeing 747-338 in 1989. (*Author*)

A British Airways BAC111 at the runway 27 right holding point. (*Author*)

Pan Am's 747-121s are there, along with a company Airbus A310 and a single Boeing 727-221 operating a feeder service, probably from Germany. TWA, Air India, Air Canada, and Brazil's Varig are represented; Air Canada have a 747 and a long-range TriStar 500 parked. Just visible through the mist is Terminal 2, with its European carriers crammed into its gates, and beyond that, Terminal 4, still only three years old, with its row of British Airways 747-236 Jumbo Jets—a nickname deplored by the purist, but one that has stuck. On the far side of the airport is the cargo area. We go past the Perry Oaks sewage works and the threshold of runway 09 right as we pass directly over its opposite, 09 left.

The aircraft turns tightly to the left, and as we bank steeply, again, just visible through the mist, Heathrow lies spread out behind the DC9 and to the aircraft's left. We go over Staines and the reservoirs that supply water to a large area around here, the airport included. Continuing to turn and climb, the airport passes by, the left-hand window seat giving a good view of Heathrow, albeit a little obscured by the mist. The route to our destination will take us higher than the aircraft approaching Heathrow's runway 27 left, over the Green Man pub and right past the little park at Myrtle Avenue, just to the side of 27 left's threshold and adjoining the Great Southwest Road, where this morning, even if it is a little misty, spotters and photographers gather as the arriving aircraft glide by, seemingly almost within touching distance. It's also where, decades before this morning's flight, Brigadier-General Critchley, then the head of BOAC, had commented on a new home base for his airline, and where even before that, Richard Fairey had used the main road to access Cain's Lane and his test airfield. At 3 p.m. this afternoon, the use of runways will change; landings will then be on 27 right, departures on 27 left, giving local residents a rest from the noise of jet engines. Over London, and the sights below become harder to see. The mist presents no problem for the controllers in Heathrow's tower, the ground movements radar showing where every aircraft and vehicle is on the airport. Now, our ascending aircraft is controlled by air traffic controllers at West Drayton, just north of Heathrow, our position clearly shown on their radar screens.

Crystal-clear sunny days are perfect for aviation enthusiasts when passing by an airport like Heathrow. If the mist was not hanging over south-east England today, the view would enable the approaching and departing aircraft to see the sights of London now some way below, those that have been there since long before Heathrow came along. This particular morning, as the DC9-30 climbs over London and points its nose towards the coast and Amsterdam, it's too misty.

Today, over twenty-five years after that departure, the same route no longer sees British Midland Airways flying to Amsterdam, or to anywhere else. They are now part of Heathrow's past, as are Pan Am, TWA, and a host of other airlines that have arrived and departed, known of now only in books and in photographs. Also gone is the Douglas DC9-30. Today's flight to Amsterdam would be by British Airways or KLM Royal Dutch Airlines. Both flew the route in 1989 and for years before that.

In 2016, a British Airways Airbus A319, A320, or A321 would probably be used, and it would depart from Terminal 5, a runway's length away from the threshold of 27 right, so it would be a long taxi. Having got there, the aircraft will cross the holding point and turn onto the runway, face the way it has come, and, its engines noticeably

London to Amsterdam in 2016, flown by a British Airways Airbus A321. (*Author*)

Another London to Amsterdam flight in 2016, this time flown by a KLM Boeing 737. (*Author*)

much quieter than the DC9 as it powers along the runway, pass the gleaming edifice of the new Terminal 2, The Queen's Terminal, past the steadily reducing shell of the now closed Terminal 1, once the largest single airport terminal in Europe. The aircraft will still lift off the runway more or less where the tunnel is, still, for now at least, soar past Terminal 3, past the airport's new and much taller control tower, and past the Boeing 777s, Boeing 787 Dreamliners, Airbus A350s, and gargantuan shapes of Airbus A380s that now ply the world's air routes to the UK capital. Then it will pass the terminal just departed from, Terminal 5, the sewage works just a memory.

The left turn will still be over Staines. The air traffic control centre at West Drayton is now another memory, replaced by a state-of-the-art facility at Swanwick. However, as the aircraft climbs, the view of the runways and terminals will still be there, the shape now of a linear nature, the Star of David runway pattern, the diamond-shaped central area another ever-increasingly distant recollection of the past. The Myrtle Avenue Park remains, as do its airliner enthusiasts, the Green Man, and the Great Southwest Road. London is still there, as is its airport. Whoever owns it, whoever runs it, and whoever is licensed to operate it, the airport has endured, and it will remain unapologetically, defiantly, Heathrow.

You are departing from and flying above seventy years (and counting) of history.

Leaving—an Air Canada Boeing 777. (*Author*)

Leaving—a Thai Airways Airbus A340. (*Author*)

A British Airways Boeing 747-436. (*Tyler McDowell*)

The tower, the spotter, and a British Airways Boeing 747-436. (*Leo Martin*)

Another memory of the past—the old radar tower. (*Author*)

The Heathrow Express to London. (*Author*)

The station. (Author)

London Paddington. (*Author*)

Key Facts and Figures

Figures for 2014, the last full year before the closure of Terminal 1 in mid-2015.

Airport area   1,227 hectares

Terminal 1   opened 1968
Terminal 2   opened 2014
Terminal 3   opened 1961
Terminal 4   opened 1986
Terminal 5   opened 2008

Number of flights   470,665
Daily Average   1,290

Contact Stands   125
Remote Stands   49
Cargo Stands   12

Number of Airlines   80

Destinations   185 in 84 countries

Most Popular Destinations:

1 New York
2 Dubai
3 Dublin
4 Hong Kong
5 Frankfurt

Number of Passengers   73.4 million
Busiest ever year   2014

Percentage of Passengers:

International	93 per cent	(68.1 million)
Domestic	7 per cent	(5.3 million)

Business Passengers	30 per cent	(22.2 million)
Leisure Passengers	70 per cent	(51.2 million)
Transfer Passengers	36 per cent	(26.3 million)

Passenger Volume by Terminal:

Terminal 1	9.8 million	(81,696 flights)
Terminal 2	6.2 million	(41,481 flights)
Terminal 3	16.6 million	(82,801 flights)
Terminal 4	9.2 million	(54,567 flights)
Terminal 5	31.6 million	(207,859 flights)

July 2015 was a month of personal bests for Heathrow, with a record 7.29 million passengers (an increase of 4.7 per cent on July 2014). For the first time ever, the airport served over 250,000 passengers, not just once but on three separate days. 31 July saw the most passengers ever travelling through Heathrow, with 254,375 passengers using the airport.

Source: Heathrow Airport Ltd.